# Comprehension Strategy Assessment

## CSA

### Second Edition

Levels Q–R/40

Grade 4

BENCHMARK EDUCATION COMPANY

**Benchmark Education Company**
145 Huguenot Street • New Rochelle, NY • 10801

Copyright © 2015 Benchmark Education Company, LLC. All rights reserved. The classroom teacher may reproduce the assessment and scoring pages in this teacher resource for individual classroom use only. The reproduction of any part of this teacher resource for an entire grade division, or entire school or school system, is strictly prohibited. No other part of this publication may be reproduced or transmitted in whole or in part in any form or by any means, electronic or mechanical, including photocopy, recording, or any information storage or retrieval system, without permission in writing from the publisher.

Common Core State Standards © Copyright 2010. National Governors Association Center for Best Practices and Council of Chief State School Officers. All rights reserved.
Printed in Guangzhou, China. 4401/0315/CA21401924

ISBN: 978-1-4900-6838-1

For ordering information, call Toll-Free 1-877-236-2465 or visit our Web site at www.benchmarkeducation.com.

## Table of Contents

**Introduction** .................................................... 4

**Directions for Administering and Scoring Assessments** ...... 5

**Pretest** ........................................................ 12

**Ongoing Comprehension Strategy Assessments** ............. 28

**Ongoing Assessments Answer Key** ......................... 30

*Comprehension Strategies*

    1–2    Analyze Character .................................. 38

    3–4    Analyze Story Elements ............................. 42

    5–6    Analyze Text Structure and Organization ............. 46

    7–8    Compare and Contrast .............................. 50

    9–10   Draw Conclusions .................................. 54

   11–12   Evaluate Author's Purpose .......................... 58

   13–14   Evaluate Fact and Opinion .......................... 62

   15–16   Identify Cause and Effect ........................... 66

   17–18   Identify Main Idea and Supporting Details ........... 70

   19–20   Identify Sequence of Events ........................ 74

   21–22   Interpret Figurative Language ....................... 78

   23–24   Make Inferences ................................... 82

   25–26   Make Judgments .................................. 86

   27–28   Make Predictions .................................. 90

   29–30   Summarize Information ............................ 94

   31–32   Use Graphic Features ............................... 98

   33–34   Use Text Features ................................. 102

*Word Study Strategies*

   35–36   Use Word Structures to Determine Word Meaning ... 106

   37–38   Use Context Clues to Determine Word Meaning .... 110

   39–40   Identify Synonyms, Antonyms, and Homonyms .... 114

   41–42   Identify Multiple-Meaning Words ................. 118

**Midyear Test** ................................................ 122

**Posttest** .................................................... 138

   Answer Sheet ........................................... 154

   Individual Scoring Charts ............................... 155

   Group Pretest/Midyear Test/Posttest Comparison Chart .... 158

   Ongoing Strategy Assessment Record .................... 159

   Common Core State Standards and Virginia SOL Correlations ........ 160

## Introduction

*Comprehension Strategy Assessment* provides assessments for measuring students' grasp of comprehension strategies in both reading and listening. Information from these assessments can be used to support instruction.

**This book contains three types of assessments:**

- The **Pretest** is designed to assess students' reading comprehension strategies at the beginning of the school year. It contains a series of seven reading passages, both fiction and nonfiction, with a total of thirty-six multiple-choice items. Information from the Pretest can be used to help plan instruction, make curriculum decisions, and select reading materials to match students' needs. Pretest scores can also be used as baseline data for evaluating students' progress from the beginning of the school year to the end.

- **Ongoing Comprehension Strategy Assessments** are focused, two-page assessments to be administered periodically during the school year. Each assessment includes a reading passage and a set of five test items to measure one specific strategy. There are two assessments per strategy, and they are intended to be used to monitor students' progress. They may be administered after completing instruction in particular strategies, or they may be administered at other appropriate times, such as at the end of each grading period. These pages may be used as reading assessments or listening assessments.

- The Midyear and Posttests are parallel to the Pretest. They contain the same number of reading passages and items as the Pretest and test the same strategies. The **Midyear Test** can be administered as a formative assessment. The results can be used to adjust instruction to improve student learning. The **Posttest** is designed to be administered at the end of the school year as a final evaluation of students' progress in comparison to their performance at the beginning of the year.

The next few pages in this book provide directions for administering and scoring the assessments and using the assessment results. Answer keys for all of the assessments can be found at the beginning of each section. Scoring Charts for scoring the assessments and recording results can be found on pages 155–157.

## DIRECTIONS FOR ADMINISTERING AND SCORING ASSESSMENTS

All of the assessments in this book may be administered to students individually or in a group. We recommend administering the Pretest, Midyear Test, and Posttest to all students at the same time. The Ongoing Comprehension Strategy Assessments may be administered in the same way, or they may be administered individually or in small groups to different students at different times. Detailed guidelines for administering and scoring each type of assessment are presented below.

## GUIDELINES FOR USING THE PRETEST

The Pretest is fourteen pages long. It includes seven one-page reading passages and a set of multiple-choice questions for each passage: thirty-six items total. These thirty-six items measure seven "clusters" of strategies and skills (as listed on the Scoring Chart, page 155) with at least four items per cluster. Each cluster includes two or more strategies grouped by similarities. For example, "Identify Main Idea and Supporting Details" and "Summarize Information" are grouped together in one cluster because they involve similar thinking skills (distinguishing essential from nonessential information). Each cluster has been labeled with a title that reflects the key thinking skill, such as "Distinguishing Important Information."

Plan for about an hour to administer the Pretest, but allow more time if needed. Students should be allowed to finish answering every question. Depending on the students and your situation, you may want to administer the Pretest in two parts in different sittings.

## To Administer the Pretest:

**1.** Make a copy of the test and Answer Sheet for each student.

**2.** Have students write their name and the date at the top of each test page.

**3.** Read the directions on the first page and make sure students know what to do.

**4.** Have students read each passage and answer the questions that go with it.

**5.** For each multiple-choice question, instruct students to choose the best answer and fill in the bubble beside the answer they choose.

**6.** Option: If you prefer, you may copy the answer sheet on page 154 of this book and have students fill in the answers on the answer sheet.

**7.** When students have finished, collect the tests and Answer Sheets.


## To Score the Pretest:

**1.** Make a copy of the Individual Pretest Scoring Chart (see page 155) for each student.

**2.** Refer to the Pretest Answer Key on page 13. It gives the letter of the correct response to each question.

**3.** Mark each question correct or incorrect on the test page (or on the answer sheet).

**4.** To find the total test score, count the number of items answered correctly.

**5.** To score by cluster, use the Individual Pretest Scoring Chart. Circle the number of each item answered correctly. The item numbers are organized by clusters of tested skills.

**6.** For each cluster on the scoring chart, add the number of items answered correctly (for example, three of four). Write the number correct in the right-hand column under Pretest Score.

## Using the Results:

1. Use the results of the Pretest to determine each student's current level of reading ability, as well as his or her proficiencies in the strategies being tested.

2. As explained earlier, the items in the Pretest measure strategies in particular clusters. A student's score on a particular cluster can pinpoint specific instructional needs. A student who answers two or more items in a skill cluster incorrectly may need focused instructional attention on those particular strategies.

3. Plotting scores on the Individual Scoring Charts and Group Pretest/Midyear Test/Posttest Comparison Chart provides a handy reference for monitoring students' growth and development. Such information can be used to identify the skills and strategies to be reinforced for a whole group, small group, or individual.

4. Store the Individual Scoring Charts for the Pretest, Midyear Test, and Posttest in an appropriate location for referral during the school year, and for end-of-year comparison of Pretest and Posttest scores.

## GUIDELINES FOR USING THE ONGOING COMPREHENSION STRATEGY ASSESSMENTS

In this program, Grade 4 covers twenty-one comprehension and word study strategies in seven skill clusters. In this book you will find two assessments for each strategy (arranged in order by strategy within Comprehension and Word Study Strategies). The assessments are numbered 1–42, and each assessment is two pages long.

The purpose of these assessments is to determine how well students have learned each strategy. You may want to administer the two strategy-based assessments at set times of the year (such as during the second and third quarters), or you can administer an assessment for a specific strategy just after teaching the strategy in the classroom. Although the assessments are numbered sequentially 1 through 42, they do not need to be administered in any set order. You may choose to assess any strategy in whatever order you teach them.

Each Ongoing Comprehension Strategy Assessment comprises a one-page reading passage and a set of five questions. For comprehension and vocabulary strategies, three of the items are multiple-choice questions; the other two are short-answer questions that require students to write their own answers. Most of these responses will be one to three sentences long. For assessments of word study strategies, all five items are multiple-choice.

Plan for fifteen to twenty minutes to administer an Ongoing Comprehension Strategy Assessment, but allow more time if needed.

*To Administer an Ongoing Assessment:*

1. Make a copy of the assessment for each student.

2. Have students write their name and the date at the top of each test page.

3. Direct students to read each passage and answer the questions that go with it.

4. For each multiple-choice question, instruct students to choose the best answer and fill in the bubble beside the answer they choose.

5. For short-answer questions, have students write their responses (in phrases or complete sentences) on the lines provided.

### Listening Comprehension

Ongoing Comprehension Strategy Assessments 1–34 are intended primarily for use as written assessments of reading comprehension. However, they may also be used as measures of listening comprehension. To use them for listening purposes, read the passage aloud to the student(s) and have the student(s) answer the questions. Students may respond by marking and writing their answers on the test page, or you may have students give oral responses. If preferred, you may use one of the two Ongoing Comprehension Strategy Assessments for reading comprehension and the other for listening comprehension.

*To Score an Ongoing Assessment:*

1. Refer to the appropriate Answer Key (see pages 30–37). The Answer Key gives the letter of the correct response for each multiple-choice question. It gives a sample correct response for each short-answer question.

2. Mark each question correct or incorrect on the test page. You may need to interpret the student's written responses and decide whether they are correct or incorrect, based on the sample answers in the Answer Key.

3. To find the total score, count the number of items answered correctly.

*Using the Results:*

1. Use the results of the Ongoing Comprehension Strategy Assessments to evaluate each student's understanding of the tested strategy or skill.

2. A student who understands and applies a given strategy should answer at least four of the five items correctly. A student who answers correctly fewer than four items may need additional instruction on a particular strategy.

3. Use the Ongoing Strategy Assessment Record to keep track of a student's scores on the assessments during the school year. The record provides space for writing the score on each of the two strategy assessments, and for noting comments relevant to a student's progress in learning a particular strategy.

## GUIDELINES FOR USING THE MIDYEAR AND POSTTESTS

The Midyear and Posttests contain the same number of reading passages and items as the Pretest and should be administered and scored in the same way. The items on these tests measure the same skills as the Pretest with the same number of items in each skill cluster. Thus, students' scores on the three tests can be compared using the Group Pretest/Midyear Test/Posttest Comparison Chart on page 158.

Use the results of the Midyear Test to pinpoint specific instructional needs. A student who answers two or more items in a skill cluster incorrectly may need focused instructional attention on those particular comprehension or word study strategies.

Use the results of the Posttest to determine each student's current level of reading ability, as well as his or her proficiencies in the strategies being tested. Compare the student's scores on the Pretest and Posttest—and on each strategy cluster within the tests—to evaluate the student's progress since the beginning of the year.

## COMPREHENSION STRATEGY ASSESSMENTS ONLINE

The Comprehension Strategy Assessments are also available online. The online tests can be administered on any device, including desktop computers, laptops, and tablets. They give students valuable experience with online testing, and offer teachers robust data-driven assessment with reporting by classroom, grade, school, and district.

## Pretest

**The Peanut** .................................................. 14

**Disappearing Treasures** ................................. 16

**Annalise's Journal** ........................................ 18

**Born to Play** ................................................. 20

**Tsunami!** ....................................................... 22

**Everyday Hero** .............................................. 24

**Johnnycakes** ................................................. 26

# Pretest Answer Key

1. D
2. A
3. D
4. B
5. C
6. C
7. B
8. A
9. D
10. B
11. A
12. D
13. C
14. A
15. B
16. B
17. A
18. C
19. B
20. D
21. C
22. A
23. B
24. A
25. D
26. D
27. C
28. D
29. B
30. A
31. B
32. D
33. C
34. A
35. A
36. D

**Pretest**

Name _____ Date _____

Directions: Read the passage. Then use the information from the passage to answer questions 1–5.

# The Peanut

One morning in late summer, Squirrel spotted a peanut lying on the ground and ran to get it. But just as he was about to scoop it up, Bird <u>grabbed</u> the peanut in her beak. Then she flew to a branch high up in the tree.

"Hey, STOP!" yelled Squirrel. "I saw that peanut first, and it's mine!"

Bird told Squirrel, "You might have seen the peanut first, but I got it before you!"

Squirrel ran up the tree, quicker than lightning, but Bird flew higher up in the tree. Squirrel immediately climbed after her and finally grabbed the peanut from Bird's beak.

Bird didn't even flinch as she snapped it back and flew away even higher. Squirrel followed her and snatched the peanut again. Bird knocked it from Squirrel's paw and flew safely away to the next tree.

"You can't fly away from me, Bird!" Squirrel said. "I can go wherever you go!"

For the next two hours, that's exactly what he did. Bird flew and flew from branch to branch, and Squirrel ran and ran, flitting from tree to tree. The peanut went from Bird to Squirrel and from Squirrel to Bird.

After two hours, both animals were exhausted. They were <u>famished</u>, too, since neither of them ever had the chance to eat the peanut.

Finally, Squirrel got too tired to continue and stopped chasing Bird. He said, "I have a fantastic idea."

Bird was tired, too, and would have done just about anything to stop flying. So she said, "What is your great idea?"

"Why don't we each get half of the peanut?" Squirrel said. "Then we can both have a piece."

"Well, all right," Bird said, "one-half of a peanut is better than no peanut at all!"

Name _____ Date_____

1. The story says, "Bird grabbed the peanut." Which word from the story means the same as grabbed?
   - Ⓐ knocked
   - Ⓑ spotted
   - Ⓒ climbed
   - Ⓓ snatched

2. Why did Bird and Squirrel run and fly from tree to tree and branch to branch?
   - Ⓐ They were waiting for two hours to eat the peanut.
   - Ⓑ They were trying to get the peanut to the top.
   - Ⓒ They were trying to keep the peanut away from each other.
   - Ⓓ They were looking for food to eat.

3. Which words best describe the characters of both Bird and Squirrel in this story?
   - Ⓐ silly and funny
   - Ⓑ playful and quick
   - Ⓒ easily discouraged
   - Ⓓ not willing to give up

4. What is the problem in this story?
   - Ⓐ Squirrel cannot catch Bird in the trees.
   - Ⓑ Both Bird and Squirrel think they should have the peanut.
   - Ⓒ Bird cannot escape from Squirrel.
   - Ⓓ Both Bird and Squirrel want to live in a nest in the same tree.

5. The story says, "They were famished." What does famished mean?
   - Ⓐ proud
   - Ⓑ thirsty
   - Ⓒ very hungry
   - Ⓓ tired

©2015 Benchmark Education Company, LLC

**Pretest**

Name _____ Date _____

Directions: Read the passage. Then use the information from the passage to answer questions 6–10.

# Disappearing Treasures

**April 10, 1912**

It was a great day when the *Titanic* set sail from Southampton, England, and headed toward New York. The ship was like a floating hotel. It was the largest boat ever built, and more than 2,200 people were aboard. Everyone said this special ship could never <u>sink</u>.

**April 15, 1912**

Five days passed. On a cool night, the ship glided smoothly through the black water. All was quiet. Then a sailor saw trouble and yelled, "Iceberg right ahead!"

At 11:40 P.M., tragedy struck as the ship hit an iceberg. Three hours later, the *Titanic* sank and took about 1,500 people with her.

The ship that couldn't sink was lost.

**Robert Ballard's Discovery**

The *Titanic* wasn't lost forever. Many years later, in 1985, an explorer named Robert Ballard found it. He used a small submarine to look at the ship's remains. He went down 12,500 feet. That's over two miles deep!

The ship was broken into pieces. As he looked closer, he saw three large combs and a pair of child's shoes. He saw dishes, gold coins, and a bathtub. Ballard took pictures but left everything behind as it was. Soon other people wanted to see the shipwreck, too.

**The *Titanic* Today**

Time hasn't been kind to the *Titanic*. Rust drips over the windows, and the metal is <u>dissolving</u>. The *Titanic* is melting away.

Time isn't the only thing hurting the ship. Now people are harming it, too. Trash litters the sea floor, and black holes cover the top of the ship where people have landed on the wreck. Worse still, thieves have looted the ship.

Today Ballard works to save what's left. One day it will disappear, but until then, Ballard wants to protect the wreck. He thinks it's the largest museum on Earth. He says there are "many treasures yet to be found."

Name _____ Date _____

6. **What is the main idea of the first paragraph in this passage?**
   - Ⓐ The *Titanic* hit an iceberg and sank on April 10, 1912.
   - Ⓑ A hotel called the *Titanic* was completed on April 10, 1912.
   - Ⓒ The *Titanic* set sail from England on April 10, 1912.
   - Ⓓ Tragedy struck at 11:40 P.M. on April 10, 1912

7. **The passage says, "This special ship could never sink." Which of these sentences uses the word sink in the same way?**
   - Ⓐ Wash your hands in the sink before lunch.
   - Ⓑ If we don't plug the hole, this rowboat will sink.
   - Ⓒ We need to sink a post right here in the ground.
   - Ⓓ As the silence continued, Maria's confidence began to sink.

8. **What would be another good title for this passage?**
   - Ⓐ "The *Titanic*: Lost Then Found"
   - Ⓑ "Robert Ballard's Life"
   - Ⓒ "The Sailing of the *Titanic*"
   - Ⓓ "The Day Tragedy Struck"

9. **From Robert Ballard's view, what is probably the worst thing that has happened to the *Titanic* since 1985?**
   - Ⓐ Rust has dripped over the windows.
   - Ⓑ People have left trash near the wreck.
   - Ⓒ Small submarines have landed on the deck.
   - Ⓓ Thieves have taken things from the ship.

10. **The passage says, "The metal is dissolving." What does dissolving mean?**
    - Ⓐ coming back again
    - Ⓑ breaking apart and disappearing
    - Ⓒ finding an answer
    - Ⓓ slowly moving to another place

# Pretest

Name _____ Date _____

Directions: Read the passage. Then use the information from the passage to answer questions 11–15.

# Annalise's Journal

**March 1** • I'm so thrilled! After suffering with the flu for a week, I went back to school today. It was terrific seeing my friends again! The only drawback is that I still can't play soccer because I just don't feel well enough. Ronaldo says I'll get my strength back eventually, but what does a brother know?

**March 8** • I returned to soccer practice today, but I played badly. I experienced shortness of breath the first time I ran hard. After twenty minutes, the coach took me out to rest. I've already missed four games, and the team depends on me! I'm not the best player, but I am an important part of the team. The championship tournament starts in three days, and I want to contribute.

**March 9** • Most of the time Ronaldo is a nuisance, but not tonight. We ate Chinese take-out food for dinner, and when I opened my fortune cookie, I found a handwritten note inside. It said, "What was weak is now strong. Play hard, Annalise, and you'll be a champ." I looked at Ronaldo, but he just looked away and smiled.

**March 10** • For the first time this month, there's no game and no practice today, so we can all rest. Great, I say!

**March 11** • WE WON! Best of all, I was the player who scored the tie-breaking goal in the last five seconds! That shot flew into the goal like an arrow! When the game was over, my teammates hugged me so hard I thought I would faint! It was a great feeling. Tomorrow we are in the finals, and I just hope I play as well as I did today. Maybe Ronaldo was right about my strength because I'm back in the groove!

Name _____ Date _____

11. What will most likely happen tomorrow?
    Ⓐ Annalise will play in the finals.
    Ⓑ Annalise will get sick again.
    Ⓒ Ronaldo will play in the finals.
    Ⓓ Ronaldo will give Annalise another fortune cookie.

12. Why was Annalise glad to be back in school?
    Ⓐ She did not want to get the flu again.
    Ⓑ She wanted to go to soccer practice.
    Ⓒ She could not stand her brother.
    Ⓓ She had missed her friends.

13. Who wrote the note that was in the fortune cookie?
    Ⓐ Annalise
    Ⓑ her coach
    Ⓒ Ronaldo
    Ⓓ a Chinese baker

14. How was March 10 different from the other days?
    Ⓐ There was no game or practice that day.
    Ⓑ Annalise was not allowed to practice that day.
    Ⓒ The team was playing for the championship that day.
    Ⓓ Annalise and Ronaldo had Chinese food that day.

15. The end of the story says, "That shot flew into the goal like an arrow!" What does this sentence mean?
    Ⓐ The shot passed by the goal.
    Ⓑ The shot hit its target.
    Ⓒ The shot went in the wrong direction.
    Ⓓ The shot won the game.

# Pretest

Name _____  Date _____

Directions: Read the passage. Then use the information from the passage to answer questions 16–20.

# Born to Play

Lang Lang's parents wanted their son to play the piano. Before he was two, they bought him a piano for $300. That was half the money they earned that year, but it paid off. Today Lang Lang is a great <u>pianist</u>.

## Baby Genius

Lang was born in Shenyang, China. When he was only two, he was watching *Tom and Jerry* on television. It was a funny show about a cat and mouse chasing each other, and he laughed at the cartoon. He also listened to the show's music, and he liked what he heard. So little Lang walked over to the piano. His parents were amazed when he played the song perfectly!

Was Lang a genius? They would soon find out.

Lang took piano lessons. When he was five, he won a piano competition. Four years later, he moved to Beijing and began working very hard. He got up every day at 5:00 A.M. and practiced for an hour, and then he went to school. After school, he practiced piano again and then did his homework. Sometimes he had time to play with his friends. He enjoyed playing soccer or Ping-Pong.

## Teenage Sensation

When he was fifteen, Lang came to the United States, and many people noticed. In 2003, *Teen Magazine* said he was one of the "top twenty teens who will change the world."

Today Lang lives in Philadelphia. He travels all over the world to play the piano, and audiences love watching him. He plays like an angel and clearly loves what he does.

His mother would say that he was born to play.

Name _____ Date _____

16. The passage says, "Today Lang Lang is a great <u>pianist</u>." The word <u>pianist</u> means _____.

   Ⓐ like a piano

   Ⓑ person who plays the piano

   Ⓒ without a piano

   Ⓓ before the arrival of a piano

17. Information in this passage is organized mainly by _____.

   Ⓐ time order

   Ⓑ questions and answers

   Ⓒ problems and solutions

   Ⓓ causes and effects

18. Which sentence from the passage states an opinion?

   Ⓐ Lang was born in Shenyang, China.

   Ⓑ He was watching *Tom and Jerry*.

   Ⓒ It was a funny show.

   Ⓓ He also listened to the show's music.

19. Why did Lang Lang become a great piano player?

   Ⓐ His parents bought him a piano before he was two.

   Ⓑ He was born with talent and he worked hard.

   Ⓒ He moved to Beijing and got a new job.

   Ⓓ The piano he used cost $300.

20. The passage says, "He plays like an angel." What does this sentence mean?

   Ⓐ He flies all over the world.

   Ⓑ He has wings.

   Ⓒ He also plays a harp.

   Ⓓ He plays very well.

# Pretest

Name _____ Date_____

Directions: Read the passage. Then use the information from the passage to answer questions 21–25.

# Tsunami!

On that Sunday morning in December 2004, a huge wave in the Indian Ocean was moving toward shore. By the time it reached the beach, it was more than a wave. It was a tsunami!

## What Causes a Tsunami?

What is a tsunami? How does it form? Let's take a look at the 2004 tsunami that hit several parts of Asia. It started with an earthquake. The quake pushed water up toward the surface, and the wave began moving toward shore. The wave gathered speed and soon got closer to land. Then it slowed down, but at the same time it grew higher. Last, the wave hit the shore.

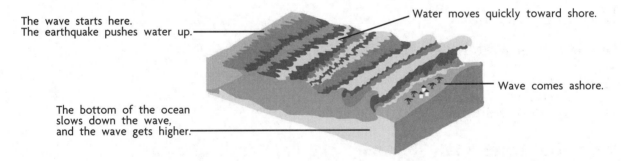

## Effects of a Tsunami

A tsunami destroys almost everything in its path. Waves crash against the shore and smash buildings. Whole towns are destroyed.

In the 2004 tsunami, more than 200,000 people died, and many more were missing. People lost their homes, their loved ones, and their farms and stores. A tsunami is a great disaster.

| Deadliest Tsunamis | | |
|---|---|---|
| Date | Location | Lives Lost |
| Dec. 26, 2004 | Indian Ocean | 200,000+ |
| Nov. 1, 1755 | Atlantic Ocean | 60,000 |
| May 22, 1782 | Pacific Ocean | 40,000 |
| Aug. 27, 1883 | Indian Ocean | 36,500 |
| Sept. 20 1498 | Pacific Ocean | 31,000 |

Name _____ Date _____

21. Which is the best summary of this passage?
    Ⓐ  Both the causes and effects of a tsunami can be deadly.
    Ⓑ  A tsunami is a series of waves that move toward shore.
    Ⓒ  Tsunamis are caused by earthquakes and can be deadly, like the one in 2004.
    Ⓓ  In 2004 a tsunami hit parts of Asia.

22. In what part of the passage should you look to find out what a tsunami does to the land?
    Ⓐ  **Effects of a Tsunami**
    Ⓑ  **What Causes a Tsunami?**
    Ⓒ  **Deadliest Tsunamis**
    Ⓓ  the first paragraph

23. What causes a tsunami wave to slow down as it gets closer to shore?
    Ⓐ  the height of the wave
    Ⓑ  the bottom of the ocean
    Ⓒ  the cool surface
    Ⓓ  the wind pressure

24. Using the information from the chart, what can you conclude about the 2004 tsunami?
    Ⓐ  It was the deadliest tsunami in the last 500 years.
    Ⓑ  The 2004 tsunami did not cause a great amount of damage.
    Ⓒ  It was the only tsunami that occurred in the Indian Ocean.
    Ⓓ  The 2004 tsunami lasted longer than any other tsunami.

25. The author's purpose in this passage was to _____.
    Ⓐ  tell an entertaining story about tsunamis
    Ⓑ  teach a lesson
    Ⓒ  compare the Pacific and Indian oceans
    Ⓓ  give information

# Everyday Hero

## by Sylvia Gonzales

There are heroes in our midst, and sometimes we do not see them. Did anyone see Maud Taylor when she was eight years old? That's when she planted her first tree. Did anyone see her when she was nine? She planted her second one. Each year on her birthday, Maud planted a tree in the vacant lot next to her house.

Maud grew up in a neighborhood that used to be called "the wrong side of the tracks." Homes in her neighborhood stood unpainted. Rusty cars without tires littered backyards, and fences needed whitewash. Doing things like planting trees did not put food on the table, so people did not have time for them. But Maud was an unusual girl. She looked at the vacant lot and saw a forest.

Maud didn't have money to buy a tree when she was young, but she had a wagon and a spade. Each year she ventured far from her neighborhood to visit a forest. When she returned home, her wagon held a small seedling.

Maud still lives in the old neighborhood today. Now she has enough money to go to a nursery and, not surprisingly, each year she still plants a tree in the old vacant lot.

Last week the city bought the lot. Because of all the trees on it, city officials decided to transform it into a neighborhood park. When Maud found out, tears filled her eyes. She felt as if she had won the jackpot.

Few people know about Maud's trees, and Maud doesn't care if people know or not. She does it for the love of trees. I know, because Maud is my mother. When I turned eight years old, I went with her to the lot. This year I went with her again, and we planted her 70th tree.

Maud is an invisible hero, but I can see her. She believes that one tree can become a forest. Can you see her, too?

Name _____  Date _____

26. Maud Taylor visited a forest each year to _____.
    Ⓐ enjoy being surrounded by nature
    Ⓑ take a long walk
    Ⓒ use her wagon for something useful
    Ⓓ dig up a seedling

27. What caused Maud to cry?
    Ⓐ She did not win the jackpot.
    Ⓑ She wished people knew about her good work.
    Ⓒ She was moved that the lot would become a park.
    Ⓓ She grew up without a lot of money to spend.

28. The passage says, "City officials decided to transform it into a neighborhood park." The word transform means _____.
    Ⓐ pay for
    Ⓑ build
    Ⓒ move to another place
    Ⓓ change

29. Which sentence best describes the character of Maud Taylor?
    Ⓐ She lives in the wrong neighborhood.
    Ⓑ She does not call attention to herself.
    Ⓒ She knows a lot about gardening.
    Ⓓ She does not get involved in her community.

30. The author probably wrote this passage because she _____.
    Ⓐ was proud of her mother and wanted people to know about her
    Ⓑ thought her mother would want people to know what she did
    Ⓒ didn't want people to think the trees just grew in the city on their own
    Ⓓ wanted the city to pay for the trees

# Pretest

Name _____ Date _____

Directions: Read the passage. Then use the information from the passage to answer questions 31–36.

# Johnnycakes

Early settlers in America ate cornmeal like it was going out of style. Corn was easily grown in most places, and it filled you up. Served with beans, it is a good source of protein.

Cornmeal is made from dry corn that has been <u>ground</u>. Back then, corn kernels were placed in a wooden bowl or a hollow tree stump and pounded into powder—usually by young boys.

When people had maple syrup, they made johnnycakes. Johnnycakes and maple syrup fit together like a hand and a glove. Here's how to make this cornmeal treat. (Ask an adult to help.)

**You'll Need:**
3/4 cup cornmeal
1 cup flour
1 tablespoon baking powder
1/2 teaspoon salt
3 tablespoons maple syrup
2 tablespoons oil
1 egg
1 cup milk

1. Mix dry ingredients in one bowl and wet ingredients in another bowl.

2. Add everything together in one bowl, and stir until the mixture is <u>moist</u>.

3. Spray a round cake pan with cooking oil, and pour batter into the pan.

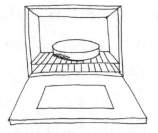

4. Bake for 25 minutes.

5. Use oven mitts to take the cake out of the oven. Let it cool for ten minutes.

6. Turn cake over onto a plate and cut into eight pie pieces. Then serve!

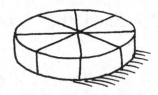

Name _____ Date_____

31. The passage says, "Early settlers in America ate cornmeal like it was going out of style." This sentence means that they _____.

    Ⓐ wore nice clothes when they ate corn
    Ⓑ ate a lot of cornmeal
    Ⓒ were afraid they would run out of corn
    Ⓓ did not know how to prepare cornmeal

32. The passage says, "Cornmeal is made from dry corn that has been ground." Which sentence uses the word ground in the same way?

    Ⓐ Put that basket on the ground.
    Ⓑ The electrician did not ground the light switch.
    Ⓒ We could not gain any ground against them.
    Ⓓ Dad ground some coffee beans for breakfast.

33. The passage says, "Johnnycakes and maple syrup fit together like a hand and a glove." This sentence means that _____.

    Ⓐ johnnycakes taste awful
    Ⓑ you should wear gloves when you make johnnycakes
    Ⓒ johnnycakes and maple syrup go together well
    Ⓓ you can call johnnycakes by different names

34. To make johnnycakes, what should you do just after putting all the ingredients into one bowl?

    Ⓐ Stir until the mixture is moist.  Ⓑ Pour the batter into a pan.
    Ⓒ Mix the dry ingredients together.  Ⓓ Bake for 25 minutes.

35. The passage says, "Stir until the mixture is moist." Which word in the passage means the opposite of moist?

    Ⓐ dry                Ⓑ filling
    Ⓒ wet                Ⓓ hollow

36. The first two paragraphs of this passage tell mostly about _____.

    Ⓐ how cornmeal was ground up
    Ⓑ how cornmeal makes delicious johnnycakes
    Ⓒ how you can make johnnycakes like the early settlers did
    Ⓓ how early settlers prepared and ate cornmeal

## Ongoing Assessments

| | | |
|---|---|---|
| Assessment 1: | **Elizabeth Cady Stanton (Biography)** <br> Analyze Character | 38 |
| Assessment 2: | **Everybody's Hero (Biography)** <br> Analyze Character | 40 |
| Assessment 3: | **The Wall (Realistic Fiction)** <br> Analyze Story Elements | 42 |
| Assessment 4: | **Special Delivery (Realistic Fiction)** <br> Analyze Story Elements | 44 |
| Assessment 5: | **Land of Ice and Snow (Informational Article)** <br> Analyze Text Structure and Organization | 46 |
| Assessment 6: | **High-Flying Dreams (Biography)** <br> Analyze Text Structure and Organization | 48 |
| Assessment 7: | **Insects for Dinner (Science Informational Text)** <br> Compare and Contrast | 50 |
| Assessment 8: | **Kangaroos and Opossums (Science Informational Text)** <br> Compare and Contrast | 52 |
| Assessment 9: | **Wise Words (Social Studies Informational Text)** <br> Draw Conclusions | 54 |
| Assessment 10: | **Pests (Social Studies Informational Text)** <br> Draw Conclusions | 56 |
| Assessment 11: | **Washington Still the Best (Editorial)** <br> Evaluate Author's Purpose | 58 |
| Assessment 12: | **Living on a Kibbutz (Social Studies Informational Text)** <br> Evaluate Author's Purpose | 60 |
| Assessment 13: | **The Mystery of Stonehenge (Social Studies Informational Text)** <br> Evaluate Fact and Opinion | 62 |
| Assessment 14: | **The Sox and the Bambino (Informational Article)** <br> Evaluate Fact and Opinion | 64 |
| Assessment 15: | **Sailing to California (Social Studies Informational Text)** <br> Identify Cause and Effect | 66 |
| Assessment 16: | **Saving Joseph (Science Informational Text)** <br> Identify Cause and Effect | 68 |
| Assessment 17: | **The Lost Colony (Social Studies Informational Text)** <br> Identify Main Idea and Supporting Details | 70 |
| Assessment 18: | **A New Kind of Studio (Informational Article)** <br> Identify Main Idea and Supporting Details | 72 |
| Assessment 19: | **Sail Away (How-To Article)** <br> Identify Sequence of Events | 74 |
| Assessment 20: | **A Long Journey (Informational Article)** <br> Identify Sequence of Events | 76 |
| Assessment 21: | **Camels of the Plant World (Science Informational Text)** <br> Interpret Figurative Language | 78 |

**Assessment 22: Aunt Tallulah's Carpet (Fantasy)** .................... 80
Interpret Figurative Language

**Assessment 23: The Voice of History (Play)** ........................ 82
Make Inferences

**Assessment 24: Mapping the Pacific (Social Studies Informational Text)** ...... 84
Make Inferences

**Assessment 25: Benjamin Banneker (Biography)** ..................... 86
Make Judgments

**Assessment 26: A Life in Pictures (Biography)** ..................... 88
Make Judgments

**Assessment 27: A Backward Look (Fantasy)** ........................ 90
Make Predictions

**Assessment 28: Sally Ride, Scientist and Space Explorer (Biography)** ........ 92
Make Predictions

**Assessment 29: Calendars (Math Informational Text)** ................. 94
Summarize Information

**Assessment 30: Modern Ranching (Informational Article)** ............. 96
Summarize Information

**Assessment 31: What You Hear (Science Informational Text)** ................. 98
Use Graphic Features

**Assessment 32: The Underground Railroad (Social Studies Informational Text)** .... 100
Use Graphic Features

**Assessment 33: Where Would We Go Without Roads? (Informational Article)** ..... 102
Use Text Features

**Assessment 34: Exploring the Deep (Science Informational Text)** ............ 104
Use Text Features

**Assessment 35: Comets and Meteors (Science Informational Text)** ........... 106
Use Word Structures to Determine Word Meaning

**Assessment 36: Bird Food (Science Informational Text)** ................... 108
Use Word Structures to Determine Word Meaning

**Assessment 37: Magic Math Figures (Math Informational Text)** ............. 110
Use Context Clues to Determine Word Meaning

**Assessment 38: Surviving Winter (Science Informational Text)** ............. 112
Use Context Clues to Determine Word Meaning

**Assessment 39: Underground Buildings (Informational Article)** ............. 114
Identify Synonyms, Antonyms, and Homonyms

**Assessment 40: The Power of Magma (Science Informational Text)** .......... 116
Identify Synonyms, Antonyms, and Homonyms

**Assessment 41: Windmills (Science Informational Text)** .................. 118
Identify Multiple-Meaning Words

**Assessment 42: Growing Spuds (How-To Article)** ....................... 120
Identify Multiple-Meaning Words

**Assessment 1: Elizabeth Cady Stanton**
(Analyze Character)
1. B
2. D
3. C
4. Example: None of the women delegates at the World's Anti-Slavery Convention got a seat.
5. Examples: She led the women's rights convention. She wrote and presented statements for a Declaration of Rights.

**Assessment 2: Everybody's Hero**
(Analyze Character)
1. C
2. B
3. D
4. Examples: He cared about people. He was determined to help the people of Nicaragua.
5. Examples: He made it to the major leagues. He became one of the top players. He decided to get food to Nicaragua and lost his life trying.

**Assessment 3: The Wall**
(Analyze Story Elements)
1. C
2. A
3. D
4. Example: Persa smiled at Gwen and told her she did a good job.
5. Example: She felt clumsy at the beginning but more confident at the end.

**Assessment 4: Special Delivery**
(Analyze Story Elements)
1. B
2. A
3. A
4. Example: She had to wait two weeks before she could visit her grandmother, and she had nothing to do.
5. Example: She went to work with her father and volunteered to deliver some building plans.

**Assessment 5: Land of Ice and Snow**
(Analyze Text Structure and Organization)
1. D
2. B
3. C
4. Example: You can see more kinds of whales and seals there. You can see emperor and Adélie penguins.
5. Example: No countries own Antarctica. They have agreed to share it and keep it as it is.

**Assessment 6: High-Flying Dreams**
(Analyze Text Structure and Organization)
1. B
2. C
3. C
4. Examples: then, during, after, later; dates, such as "In 1929."
5. Examples: She returned to racing airplanes and tested jets. She ran her business and was twice voted "Woman of the Year in Business."

**Assessment 7: Insects for Dinner**
(Compare and Contrast)
1. B
2. D
3. A
4. The sundew catches insects with sticky drops; the Venus flytrap has two-part traps that snap shut.
5. The sundew opens its arms to let the insect's remains blow away; the Venus flytrap does not need to do this because it crushes the insect's body.

**Assessment 8: Kangaroos and Opossums**
(Compare and Contrast)
1. C
2. C
3. D
4. Example: Both eat plants. Kangaroos eat mostly grass, but opossums eat leaves, fruit, bugs, and other things.
5. Example: Kangaroos spend their time on the ground; opossums spend some time in trees.

**Assessment 9: Wise Words**
(Draw Conclusions)
1. B
2. D
3. A
4. Example: If you try to do two things at once, you probably won't do either one well.
5. Example: Fleas were common in, or familiar to, both cultures.

**Assessment 10: Pests**
(Draw Conclusions)
1. D
2. B
3. C
4. Example: Zebra mussels came from outside the United States.
5. Examples: Plant seeds can travel on shoes. Animals can come in as pets. Insects can travel on airplanes, cars, or ships.

**Assessment 11: Washington Still the Best**
(Evaluate Author's Purpose)
1. C
2. C
3. B
4. Example: To show that Washington was a great leader
5. Example: The author thinks it is too bad that Washington fell so low in the polls. He should be higher because he was a great president.

**Assessment 12: Living on a Kibbutz**
(Evaluate Author's Purpose)
1. D
2. B
3. C
4. Example: The author seems to think it's a great idea. He says that everyone acted like one big family.
5. Examples: "It was a wonderful way of life!" "Life on a kibbutz today is sadly much different from in the past."

**Assessment 13: The Mystery of Stonehenge**
(Evaluate Fact and Opinion)
1. A
2. D
3. B
4. Example: The third stage went from 2,550 to 1,600 B.C.E. This statement can be verified.
5. Example: The sun shines through the stones in unusual ways when the seasons change. Ancient people worshipped the sun and moon.

**Assessment 14: The Sox and the Bambino**
(Evaluate Fact and Opinion)
1. D
2. C
3. A
4. It expresses an opinion: "a wonderful thing happened."
5. The student writes a sentence and tells whether it is a fact or an opinion.

**Assessment 15: Sailing to California**
(Identify Cause and Effect)
1. C
2. B
3. D
4. Example: The wind got stronger and the wagon gained speed going downhill.
5. Example: They got angry with Zeb Thomas and ran him out of town.

**Assessment 16: Saving Joseph**
(Identify Cause and Effect)
1. A
2. C
3. D
4. Example: Pasteur had lost three of his five children to disease, and he wanted to fight diseases.
5. Example: Joseph was cured and went on to live a full life.

**Assessment 17: The Lost Colony**
(Identify Main Idea and Supporting Details)
1. C
2. D
3. Example: A second group of colonists settled in Roanoke in 1587.
4. B
5. Examples: When he returned, the people were gone. None of the colonists were ever seen again.

**Assessment 18: A New Kind of Studio**
(Identify Main Ideas and Supporting Details)
1. C
2. A
3. B
4. Example: Lucas came up with a new way to make movies on computers.
5. Examples: Pixar's first six movies made almost $3 billion. *The Incredibles* won an Academy Award.

**Assessment 19: Sail Away**
(Identify Sequence of Events)
1. Choose ten sticks of the same length and pull off any leaves.
2. D
3. B
4. Example: Place it in water and let it sail.
5. D

**Assessment 20: A Long Journey**
(Identify Sequence of Events)
1. D
2. B
3. A
4. Example: The monarchs begin to move north again.
5. Examples: First, they lay eggs along the way. Then (or finally) they reach their summer homes.

**Assessment 21: Camels of the Plant World**
(Interpret Figurative Language)
1. D
2. A
3. B
4. Example: They both live in the desert and don't need much water.
5. Example: One kind is like a big pincushion with pins sticking out. This sentence compares a cactus to a pincushion.

**Assessment 22: Aunt Tallulah's Carpet**
(Interpret Figurative Language)
1. C
2. A
3. D
4. Example: The author uses a simile. "The objects on the floor were like big bugs wrapped in silk webs."
5. Example: "The deep reds and blues sparkled like jewels" compares the colors of the carpet to jewels.

**Assessment 23: The Voice of History**
(Make Inferences)
1. D
2. Examples: We are watching TV news; it takes place at the Lincoln Memorial; Lincoln died in 1865 and is now a "statue."
3. C
4. A
5. Example: She is surprised, frightened, excited. Her voice becomes shaky and low. She says, "Incredible!"

**Assessment 24: Mapping the Pacific**
(Make Inferences)
1. A
2. D
3. B
4. Example: It was hard to keep food fresh on long trips. They didn't have refrigerators and couldn't get fresh food if they didn't stop anywhere.
5. Example: Almost no one had been to the Pacific Ocean. People thought there might be a continent in the South Pacific and land at the South Pole, but they did not know.

**Assessment 25: Benjamin Banneker**
(Make Judgments)
1. B
2. Examples: astronomy and surveying
3. Examples: He was a skilled surveyor and could make maps.
4. A
5. C

**Assessment 26: A Life in Pictures**
(Make Judgments)
1. C
2. D
3. C
4. Example: She took pictures during wars.
5. Examples: Her plane crashed. Her ship was hit by a torpedo. Bombs fell around her.

**Assessment 27: A Backward Look**
(Make Predictions)
1. B
2. C
3. Example: She is probably Ralph's great-grandmother. She has the same last name as his grandparents.
4. Example: He would probably say that he is Ralph, not Jamie, or he might ask who she is.
5. A

**Assessment 28: Sally Ride, Scientist and Space Explorer**
(Make Predictions)
1. B
2. C
3. A
4. Examples: She would have become a scientist, a science teacher, or perhaps a writer.
5. Example: Her experience probably increased other women's chances because she paved the way and served as a role model.

**Assessment 29: Calendars**
(Summarize Information)
1. C
2. Example: The calendar we use is based on the Julian calendar of ancient Rome.
3. D
4. A
5. Example: It is the time of a full cycle of the moon from new to full and back again.

**Assessment 30: Modern Ranching**
(Summarize Information)
1. A
2. D
3. Example: Web sites on the Internet post information for ranchers on many topics.
4. A
5. Example: Ranching has changed in many ways in the past 150 years. Many ranchers today use computers and other machines.

**Assessment 31: What You Hear**
(Use Graphic Features)
1. D
2. 80 decibels
3. A
4. B
5. Examples: jet planes, sirens

**Assessment 32: The Underground Railroad**
(Use Graphic Features)
1. C
2. It was illegal to help slaves escape.
3. D
4. Slavery became illegal in new northern states.
5. C

**Assessment 33: Where Would We Go Without Roads?**
(Use Text Features)
1. D
2. B
3. C
4. Example: They were wide, straight, and deep with layers of sand and gravel.
5. Thomas Telford

**Assessment 34: Exploring the Deep**
(Use Text Features)
1. D
2. A
3. C
4. It is a deep place in the Pacific Ocean near Ecuador.
5. Example: ROVs are robots used to take pictures underwater and pick things up from the ocean floor.

**Assessment 35: Comets and Meteors**
(Use Word Structures to Determine Word Meaning)
1. C
2. D
3. B
4. A
5. B

**Assessment 36: Bird Food**
(Use Word Structures to Determine Word Meaning)
1. C
2. D
3. A
4. D
5. B

**Assessment 37: Magic Math Figures**
(Use Context Clues to Determine Word Meaning)
1. C
2. B
3. Example: The passage mentions "across" and "up and down." Diagonally must refer to another direction.
4. Example: The passage says, "It will not be easy."
5. C

**Assessment 38: Surviving Winter**
(Use Context Clues to Determine Word Meaning)
1. C
2. A
3. Examples: "special deep sleep"; "wake up again"
4. D
5. Examples: "down right on the ground"; "feet under them"

**Assessment 39: Underground Buildings**
(Identify Synonyms, Antonyms, and Homonyms)
1. C
2. B
3. A
4. D
5. C

**Assessment 40: The Power of Magma**
(Identify Synonyms, Antonyms, and Homonyms)
1. C
2. C
3. A
4. B
5. D

**Assessment 41: Windmills**
(Identify Multiple-Meaning Words)
1. C
2. D
3. B
4. A
5. A

**Assessment 42: Growing Spuds**
(Identify Multiple-Meaning Words)
1. B
2. C
3. A
4. B
5. D

# Elizabeth Cady Stanton

Today, we take it for granted that women can vote. This was not always so. Women won the right to vote, thanks to leaders like Elizabeth Cady Stanton. She fought for equal rights for women. She wanted women to have the same rights as men.

Elizabeth Cady was born in 1815. Her father was a judge. Elizabeth studied law in his office. She also studied Greek, Latin, and math. She got the best education a woman could get at the time.

After graduating from school, Cady met the man who would be her husband. His name was Henry Stanton. He worked hard to end slavery in the United States. He and Elizabeth were married in 1840. Then they went to the World's Anti-Slavery Convention in London, England. There, Cady Stanton met Lucretia Mott. Mott was denied a seat in the meeting hall. In fact, none of the women got a seat. This convinced Cady Stanton that women should hold their own meeting for women's rights.

In 1848, Cady Stanton led the first women's rights convention. It took place in Seneca Falls, New York. Cady Stanton wrote statements for a Declaration of Rights. She presented them at this meeting.

Elizabeth Cady Stanton fought for women's rights for the rest of her life. She died in 1897 at the age of 82.

Name _____ Date _____

1. For much of her life, Elizabeth Cady Stanton's main goal was to _____.
   - Ⓐ vote for a president
   - Ⓑ gain equal rights for women
   - Ⓒ become a lawyer
   - Ⓓ hold a meeting for women only

2. Based on the information in the passage, which words best describe the character of Elizabeth Cady Stanton?
   - Ⓐ angry and fierce
   - Ⓑ generous and caring
   - Ⓒ humorous and sharp
   - Ⓓ intelligent and determined

3. Which fact supports the character traits you chose in question two?
   - Ⓐ She took for granted that women could vote.
   - Ⓑ Her father was a judge and she got a good education.
   - Ⓒ She studied law and fought for women's rights.
   - Ⓓ Her husband, Henry Stanton, fought to end slavery.

4. What convinced Elizabeth Cady Stanton to hold a convention for women's rights?

   _____

   _____

5. Elizabeth Cady Stanton was considered a daring and dedicated leader. Give one or two details from the passage to support this statement.

   _____

   _____

# Everybody's Hero

Roberto Clemente was upset. It was December 1972. An earthquake had hit Nicaragua. Many people had lost everything. Other countries sent food and clothing, but these things were not reaching the people. When Roberto heard that, he got angry. Then he decided to do something about it. When Roberto put his mind on something, he always did it. He had been that way since he was a boy.

Roberto Clemente Walker grew up in Puerto Rico as the youngest of four children. He was great at track and field, but his best sport was baseball. He wanted to work his way up to the big leagues. In 1955, he signed with the Pittsburgh Pirates.

Roberto became one of the greatest players of all time. He could hit, field, throw, and run. He was the top batter in the league four times. He was the best right fielder twelve times. His team won two World Series, in 1960 and 1971. He won many other prizes. He was named Most Valuable Player in the 1971 World Series.

Roberto Clemente was a hero in all of Latin America. The people loved him, and he loved helping people.

That is why Roberto got on a plane for Nicaragua. His friends warned him against it. The plane was old, and the weather was bad. But the people there needed help. He was going to bring food and clothing to them. His mind was set, and he would not change his mind.

That was the last anybody saw of Roberto Clemente. His plane went down in a storm. Newspapers across the country ran the story on the front page. All Americans were sad. Clemente was still a young man.

It was a big loss for baseball, and a big loss for the world.

Name _____ Date _____

1. Which words best describe the character of Roberto Clemente?
   - Ⓐ kind and easygoing
   - Ⓑ angry and serious
   - Ⓒ generous and hardworking
   - Ⓓ friendly and amusing

2. When Roberto Clemente was a boy, his main goal was to _____.
   - Ⓐ win prizes in track and field
   - Ⓑ get into the big leagues
   - Ⓒ help people in Latin America
   - Ⓓ become a hero

3. In 1972, Clemente boarded the plane for Nicaragua because he wanted to _____.
   - Ⓐ get away from the people in the United States
   - Ⓑ help fly the plane through the storm
   - Ⓒ get to the baseball game on time
   - Ⓓ make sure the people got food and clothing

4. What did Roberto Clemente's effort to get to Nicaragua in 1972 show about him as a person?

   _____

   _____

5. Roberto Clemente was known as strong-minded. Give one or two details from the passage to support this idea.

   _____

   _____

Name _____ Date _____

Directions: Read the passage. Then use the information from the passage to answer questions 1–5.

# The Wall

Everyone on the field watched as Persa sprinted toward the ball. She was tiny, fierce, and fast. In her bright red jersey, she became a blur as she raced down the field and kicked the ball deep into the blue team's territory.

Gwen also ran down the field, trying to stay close to the ball. She pushed herself as hard as she could, but she still felt big and clumsy. Gwen was clearly the slowest runner on the red team. She had just reached the midfield line when Persa approached the blue team's goal. With a furious kick of the ball, Persa booted it toward the goal, but the blue team's goalie leaped into the air and made a beautiful save.

Then the goalie trotted out from the goal and passed the ball to one of her team members, Marisabel, who turned and charged up the field. Gwen started running back toward her goal.

As she neared the goalkeeper's box in front of her net, Gwen turned to face the action. Marisabel shot the ball toward the goal, but Gwen was ready. She crossed her arms and leaned back. The ball hit her with a thud and dropped to the ground, and a huge cheer rose from her team. Then a small red blur whizzed by. It was Persa smiling toward Gwen. "Good job!" she panted as she streaked by.

Gwen blocked many more shots that day, using her size and strength to advantage. By the end of the game, her teammates were shouting, "You can't get past The Wall!" Gwen grinned as she listened to the chanting of her teammates. She had found a place for herself on the team.

Name _____ Date _____

1. Where does this story take place?
   Ⓐ on a baseball field
   Ⓑ in a classroom
   Ⓒ on a soccer field
   Ⓓ in a gym

2. What is the theme of this story?
   Ⓐ Different people have different valuable skills to offer.
   Ⓑ Children should be taught to work together rather than compete with one another.
   Ⓒ A good sense of humor can help you overcome your problems.
   Ⓓ Parents push too hard for their kids to be successful at sports.

3. What was Gwen's main problem in this story?
   Ⓐ She kicked the ball and missed the net.
   Ⓑ She allowed the other team to score.
   Ⓒ She did not get along with her teammates.
   Ⓓ She felt slow and clumsy.

4. How did Persa help Gwen "find a place for herself" on the team?
   _____
   _____

5. How did Gwen's feelings about herself change from the beginning of the story to the end?
   _____
   _____

# Ongoing Comprehension Strategy Assessment • 4

Name _____ Date_____

Directions: Read the passage. Then use the information from the passage to answer questions 1–5.

# Special Delivery

Jamila always looked forward to summer vacation with Grandmother Latifa. Jamila said that every day with her was a new adventure. This summer, though, Jamila would have to wait two weeks before she could visit Grandmother Latifa. To Jamila, that two-week wait seemed like a year.

One night Jamila's father said, "You know, I had summer jobs to keep me busy when I was your age."

"So did I," her mother agreed. "Maybe you could find a job for yourself, Jamila. What job would you like?"

"Well," Jamila said, "I'd like to be a mail carrier. Every mail delivery seems like an adventure. You never know whom you will meet or what might happen along the way."

Jamila's parents decided that she would go to the office with her father every morning for the next week. On the first day, Jamila sat quietly in his office. She read magazines and drew pictures to help pass the time. On day two, Jamila tried her best to be patient, but it was not easy. Then she heard her father talking to Ms. Lee on the phone. He wanted to deliver some building plans to her, but he couldn't leave his office.

As Jamila listened, a lightbulb went on in her head. When her father hung up the phone, Jamila asked, "Can I deliver the plans to Ms. Lee for you, Dad?"

"Well," Jamila's father said with a smile, "now you will get your chance to be a mail carrier. Get ready for your first special-delivery adventure."

Name _____ Date _____

1. How did Jamila feel at the beginning of the story?
   - Ⓐ sad
   - Ⓑ restless
   - Ⓒ foolish
   - Ⓓ nervous

2. Where did Jamila go with her father?
   - Ⓐ to his office
   - Ⓑ to Grandmother Latifa's house
   - Ⓒ to Ms. Lee's office
   - Ⓓ to a summer vacation house

3. What did Jamila like to do best?
   - Ⓐ go on adventures
   - Ⓑ read books
   - Ⓒ work in an office
   - Ⓓ sit quietly

4. What was Jamila's main problem in this story?
   _____
   _____

5. How did Jamila solve her problem in the end?
   _____
   _____

©2015 Benchmark Education Company, LLC     Comprehension Strategy Assessment • Grade 4     45

Name _____ Date _____

Directions: Read the passage. Then use the information from the passage to answer questions 1–5.

# Land of Ice and Snow

Our world has seven continents, but Antarctica is quite different from the other six. Antarctica is sometimes called the "White Continent" because it is covered by snow and ice. Antarctica is colder than any other place in the world. It is also windier. It is the only continent that does not have any trees—not a single one!

**Sea Creatures**

However, that does not mean that Antarctica is empty. In fact, Antarctica has some of the world's largest populations of sea creatures.

The White Continent has nine types of whales and six kinds of seals—more than any of the other continents. Seals live and play on the beaches or on icebergs. They swim in the icy water. Elephant seals are the biggest. Their pups gain about 120 pounds in the first three weeks of life.

Then there are the birds of Antarctica. Thousands of penguins live there. It is the only place in the world where you can see emperor and Adélie penguins in the wild. Another strange and wonderful bird is the albatross. It is one of Earth's biggest birds. Its wingspan can be as wide as twelve feet. This giant bird can fly thousands of miles for food.

**Part of Our World**

Antarctica includes the South Pole, which is the bottom tip of Earth. Unlike the land on other continents, no country owns Antarctica. Several countries have claimed parts of it. They have set up research stations there. But most countries have agreed to share this unusual place. They will try to keep it clean and pure.

Name _____ Date _____

1. Most of the information in this passage is organized by _____.
   Ⓐ time order
   Ⓑ order of importance
   Ⓒ problem and solution
   Ⓓ compare and contrast

2. In this passage, the purpose of the first paragraph is to _____.
   Ⓐ describe the time and place
   Ⓑ introduce the main idea
   Ⓒ describe changes in Antarctica
   Ⓓ give the author's opinion

3. The information under "Sea Creatures" is presented mainly as _____.
   Ⓐ causes and effects
   Ⓑ problems and solutions
   Ⓒ categories and examples (descriptions)
   Ⓓ questions and answers

4. According to this passage, how is the wildlife in Antarctica different from wildlife on other continents?

   _____
   _____

5. In terms of government and politics, how is Antarctica different from the other continents?

   _____
   _____

Name _____ Date _____

Directions: Read the passage. Then use the information from the passage to answer questions 1–5.

# High-Flying Dreams

Jacqueline Cochran was born in a small town in Florida around 1910. Her parents died when she was young, and she had to work from early on. For years she dreamed of starting her own business one day. It was a big dream, but she made that dream come true. Along the way, Jackie Cochran also became one of the greatest fliers of all time.

As a young woman, Jackie Cochran worked in a beauty shop in Florida. In 1929, she moved to New York City and got a lucky break. She got a job in a beauty shop on Fifth Avenue, the center of fashion at that time. She had many rich customers. Some of them hired her to travel with them. She began to think of starting a business selling makeup and beauty products.

On one trip, Jackie met a rich man named Floyd Odlum. She told him about her dream. He advised her to learn how to fly an airplane to help her in business. She would need to move quickly from city to city.

Jackie quickly learned to fly and fell in love with flying. Starting a business could wait. Soon Jackie was racing airplanes.

Jackie had some bad luck in her first three years as a racer. Her planes kept breaking down. But in 1937, she won her first cross-country race. She was picked as the top woman flier of the year. By then, she was also running her own business selling makeup.

During World War II, Jackie joined the Army Air Corps. She tested planes and flew them overseas. Jackie won a prize for her leadership.

After the war, Jackie returned to racing planes. Later she tested jets, and she ran her business. During the 1950s, she was twice voted "Woman of the Year in Business."

Jackie Cochran died in 1980. She set many flying records in her lifetime and won many honors. Best of all, perhaps, she lived her dream.

Name _____ Date _____

1. Most of the information in this passage is organized by _____.
   - Ⓐ cause and effect
   - Ⓑ time order
   - Ⓒ problem and solution
   - Ⓓ compare and contrast

2. What is the first paragraph mostly about?
   - Ⓐ Jackie's parents
   - Ⓑ working in a beauty shop
   - Ⓒ Jackie's childhood
   - Ⓓ flying airplanes

3. What event made Jackie Cochran go in a new direction?
   - Ⓐ working in a beauty shop in Florida
   - Ⓑ racing an airplane
   - Ⓒ meeting a man who advised her to learn to fly
   - Ⓓ having her plane break down

4. Write three signal words or phrases from the passage that the author used to help describe when events took place.

   _____
   _____

5. What did Jackie Cochran do after World War II? Tell about two or three things she did.

   _____
   _____

# Insects for Dinner

The sundew and the Venus flytrap are unusual plants. They grow in swamps or bogs, which are wet places. These wet places do not supply enough minerals for plants to grow well. So the sundew and Venus flytrap catch insects for food. The insects provide all the minerals these plants need.

Sundew leaves have long tentacles, or "arms." Each arm has a sticky drop at the end. When an insect lands on a sundew leaf, it sticks. As the insect fights to get away, other arms bend toward the insect to form a trap. Next, the arms produce a special juice that breaks down the insect's body. When the food from inside the insect is eaten, the arms of the plant open. The wind blows away the part of the insect that cannot be used for food.

The Venus flytrap has two-part traps. Spikes stick out from the inside of each part, or lobe. When an insect lands on a lobe, it may touch a very sensitive trigger. If the insect touches this trigger twice, the lobes of the Venus flytrap instantly shut tight. It takes less than a second for this to occur.

As with the sundew, a special juice in the Venus flytrap breaks down the insect for food. Unlike the sundew, the Venus flytrap does not need the wind to blow away leftover insect parts. This plant crushes the insect body with the spikes inside its traps.

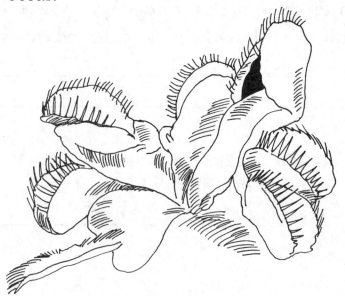

Name _____ Date _____

1. In what way are the sundew and the Venus flytrap alike?
   Ⓐ Both eat other plants.
   Ⓑ Both live in wet places.
   Ⓒ Both have long arms.
   Ⓓ Both drink special juices.

2. Both the sundew and Venus flytrap catch insects for food because they _____.
   Ⓐ do not have roots
   Ⓑ have to get exercise
   Ⓒ do not take in water
   Ⓓ need minerals to grow

3. Both the sundew and Venus flytrap produce a special juice to _____.
   Ⓐ break down the insects' bodies
   Ⓑ attract insects
   Ⓒ catch insects on their leaves
   Ⓓ absorb minerals

4. How are the sundew and Venus flytrap different in the ways they catch food?
   _____
   _____

5. What do the sundew and Venus flytrap do differently after they have digested their food?
   _____
   _____

Name _____ Date _____

Directions: Read the passage. Then use the information from the passage to answer questions 1–5.

# Kangaroos and Opossums

Kangaroos and opossums are members of the same animal family. They are alike in many ways, but they are also very different. Both animals are marsupials, so they have pouches. Marsupial mothers carry their babies in these pouches. The babies stay there for up to three months. The mothers can keep them close by and make sure they are safe. They can feed their babies anytime.

They are both warm-blooded animals. (So are people.) Their bodies stay the same temperature all the time. But they live on different sides of the world. Kangaroos come from Australia. Opossums live in the Americas.

Most opossums are about as large as a cat. Kangaroos can be as big as a football player. Some kangaroos are over six feet tall. They can weigh more than 200 pounds.

Kangaroos and opossums both eat plants. But opossums also eat meat. Kangaroos spend their time on the ground and can move around fast. They eat mainly grass. Opossums spend more time in trees. They hang from their tails. This way, they can get food that is hard to reach, but other animals can't get them. Opossums will eat almost anything. They like leaves, fruit, and other plant food. They eat bugs and snails, too.

Kangaroos sleep at night, as most animals do. But opossums come out after dark.

These animals also face danger in different ways. Kangaroos fight by boxing and kicking, but opossums roll up and play dead.

Name _____ Date _____

1. How are kangaroos and opossums alike?
   Ⓐ  Both are cold-blooded.
   Ⓑ  Both sleep at night.
   Ⓒ  Both are marsupials.
   Ⓓ  Both come from Australia.

2. How are kangaroos and opossums different?
   Ⓐ  Only kangaroos have pouches.
   Ⓑ  They are from different animal families.
   Ⓒ  They are different sizes.
   Ⓓ  Only kangaroos go out at night.

3. How are kangaroos and opossums alike?
   Ⓐ  In danger, both box and kick.
   Ⓑ  Both come out during the day.
   Ⓒ  Both lay eggs in the sand.
   Ⓓ  Both carry babies in pouches.

4. How are kangaroos and opossums alike and different in what they eat?
   _____
   _____

5. How are kangaroos and opossums different in where they usually spend their time?
   _____
   _____

# Ongoing Comprehension Strategy Assessment • 9

Name _____ Date _____

Directions: Read the passage. Then use the information from the passage to answer questions 1–5.

# Wise Words

A proverb is an old, wise saying. It is a way of summing up a lesson about life in a few clever, easy-to-remember words. Most proverbs come from long ago.

Proverbs have developed everywhere. On the surface, they seem very different from country to country. But look for the meaning inside the proverb. You'll see that all of our ancestors had the same basic lessons to teach us.

Here's an example. A Russian proverb says, "If you chase two rabbits, you will catch neither." An Arabic proverb says, "He who carries two melons in one hand is sure to drop at least one of them." In Africa, people say, "You cannot hold onto two cows' tails at once." True, you may never chase a rabbit or a cow. But you can still learn from these proverbs. They all mean that it's best to focus on one task at a time. Trying to do two things at once often means doing both poorly.

Many proverbs use insects and other animals to teach lessons about human nature. A Russian proverb says, "He got angry with fleas and threw his fur coat into the oven." A Hebrew proverb about fleas makes a very different point. It says, "He who lies down with a dog will get up with fleas."

Some proverbs say exactly what they mean. Others are little puzzles that you have to figure out. In either case, it's true that proverbs are worth knowing!

**"You cannot hold onto two cows' tails at once."**

Name _____ Date _____

1. From this passage, what can you conclude about people from long ago?
   - Ⓐ They traveled all over the world.
   - Ⓑ They had a lot of experience with animals.
   - Ⓒ They never tried to do more than they could do.
   - Ⓓ They didn't tell lies like people do today.

2. Most proverbs are probably short so that _____.
   - Ⓐ they can be translated into many languages
   - Ⓑ people can write them down
   - Ⓒ they can be collected in small books
   - Ⓓ people can remember them

3. Why are proverbs from long ago still useful to people today?
   - Ⓐ People still act much the same as they did long ago.
   - Ⓑ Proverbs come from many different countries.
   - Ⓒ People still eat melons and cook rice.
   - Ⓓ Proverbs use insects and other animals to tell stories.

4. According to proverbs, why wouldn't it be a good idea to try to type a school paper while you are talking to a friend on the phone?

   _____
   _____

5. What can you conclude from the fact that a Russian proverb and a Hebrew proverb both mention fleas?

   _____
   _____

Name _____ Date _____

Directions: Read the passage. Then use the information from the passage to answer questions 1–5.

# Pests

A pest is a plant or animal that does not live naturally in an area but somehow ends up there. Sometimes a new species arrives by accident. Sometimes it is brought to a place on purpose. These new plants and animals can cause serious problems.

At one time there were no rabbits in Australia. A man named Thomas Austin took twenty-four rabbits there in 1859. Seven years later, the number of rabbits had really grown. One of Austin's neighbors killed more than two million rabbits on his land. People called the rabbits the "gray blanket." The rabbits ate crops and left fields bare. People put up fences, but the rabbits climbed them. People shot the rabbits and used poison to kill them. At last, the rabbits were under control.

Similar events have happened in the United States. Zebra mussels were first found in 1988. By 1990, they had spread to all the Great Lakes. Today, zebra mussels can be found in more than 20 states.

Zebra mussels stop the flow of water through pipes. They ruin docks. They attach themselves to boats and prevent the boats from running. They also kill other shellfish. Because the mussels eat the same food as some other shellfish and there are so many of them, the other shellfish run out of food.

New species travel to other countries all the time. Plant seeds can enter a country easily. They can even arrive on the bottom of a person's shoe. Some animals enter as pets. Insects can come in on airplanes, cars, or ships. People have to be careful about bringing plants and animals to different areas. Introducing a new species often does more harm than good.

Name _____ Date _____

1. What conclusion about rabbits can be drawn from this passage?
   Ⓐ They are very fierce.
   Ⓑ They are hard to kill.
   Ⓒ They kill other animals.
   Ⓓ Their numbers grow very quickly.

2. What evidence supports the conclusion that Australians did not want rabbits on their land?
   Ⓐ Before 1859, there were no rabbits in Australia.
   Ⓑ People shot and poisoned rabbits.
   Ⓒ The rabbits could climb fences.
   Ⓓ The rabbits came from England.

3. What can you conclude from the description of the rabbits as a "gray blanket"?
   Ⓐ They are used to make blankets.
   Ⓑ They are very soft.
   Ⓒ They cover the ground like a blanket.
   Ⓓ There are not many rabbits.

4. What can you conclude from this passage about where zebra mussels came from?
   _____
   _____

5. What evidence supports the conclusion that keeping a new species out of the country is very hard?
   _____
   _____

Name _____  Date _____

Directions: Read the passage. Then use the information from the passage to answer questions 1–5.

# Washington Still the Best

Who was the greatest president in U.S. history? Each year on Presidents' Day, polls ask that question. Each year, the people who respond to the polls pick Abraham Lincoln first. Most years, George Washington comes in a close second.

But in two recent polls, the results were suddenly different. Washington dropped to sixth place in one poll. In the other, he came in seventh. Why? It turned out that many people had never learned about Washington, and others had just forgotten.

The truth is, George Washington was not just a great president. He was also a great leader. "First in war, first in peace, and first in the hearts of his countrymen." That is what one man long ago said of Washington. Here is what those words mean.

In the early days of the United States, the leaders argued about many things. But they always agreed about George Washington. So they asked him to lead the army against the King of England.

The U.S. army was young and often outnumbered. The men almost never had enough guns. They were often cold and hungry. At first, they lost many battles. Somehow Washington saw them through the darkest times, and they won the war in the end.

After the war, Washington went back home. Soon the leaders of the new country were arguing again. But once again, both sides agreed on one thing: Washington. So he became the first president. Some people wanted to treat him like a king and call him "Your Highness." Washington had a different idea. He said, "Call me Mr. President."

In that way, Washington set an example for all the other presidents. He was a strong leader, but he was humble. That is why he was one of the greatest U.S. presidents.

Name _____  Date_____

1. The author wrote this passage mainly to _____.
    Ⓐ  give readers information about U.S. history
    Ⓑ  tell an interesting story about George Washington's life
    Ⓒ  convince readers that Washington was a great president
    Ⓓ  explain why people should not believe what polls say

2. The main purpose of paragraphs four, five, and six is to _____.
    Ⓐ  explain how polls work
    Ⓑ  tell some funny stories about Washington as a young man
    Ⓒ  give information about George Washington
    Ⓓ  convince readers that Washington was greater than Lincoln

3. Which sentence from the passage best reveals the author's opinion of Washington?
    Ⓐ  Washington dropped to sixth place in one poll.
    Ⓑ  He was also a great leader.
    Ⓒ  It turned out that many people had never learned about Washington and others had just forgotten.
    Ⓓ  After the war, Washington went back home.

4. Why does the author of this passage tell about Washington and the American army?

    _____
    _____

5. What is the author's view of Washington placing seventh in one poll?

    _____
    _____

©2015 Benchmark Education Company, LLC          Comprehension Strategy Assessment • Grade 4   59

# Ongoing Comprehension Strategy Assessment • 12

Name _____ Date _____

Directions: Read the passage. Then use the information from the passage to answer questions 1–5.

# Living on a Kibbutz

Beginning in the late 1800s, many Jews left Russia seeking freedom. They went to Palestine. That was the homeland of the Jewish people from long ago. The Jews from Russia were poor but full of hope.

In 1909, some young Jews started a farm at a place called Degania. It was next to the Sea of Galilee. They owned and worked the land together. They decided things as a group. They all took care of one another. Degania became the first kibbutz, or group-owned farm. At first, only adults lived on the kibbutz. They cleared the land and planted crops.

Over the next few decades, the kibbutz movement grew in Palestine. Children were born. Schools had to be built. Because all adults were equal, both men and women worked in the fields. This meant that day-care centers were built for the young children. All children slept together in children's houses.

On the kibbutz, everyone acted like one big family. People ate together. They took hikes and played music together. It was a wonderful way of life!

Today, there are over 250 kibbutzim in Israel. Although the basic beliefs are the same, life on a kibbutz today is sadly much different from in the past. Children live at home with their parents. Most families stay at home for entertainment rather than do things, like folk dancing, with the rest of the group. Farming is no longer the most important thing on a kibbutz.

In the old days, everyone on a kibbutz was equal. Today, the sense of being equal has been lost.

Name _____ Date _____

1. The author of this passage told about the Jews who left Russia because he wanted to _____.
   - Ⓐ compare Russia with Palestine
   - Ⓑ explain how Palestine became Israel
   - Ⓒ describe their farms in Russia
   - Ⓓ explain how the first kibbutz began

2. The author's main purpose in writing this passage was to _____.
   - Ⓐ describe the sights and sounds of a kibbutz
   - Ⓑ give a brief history of the kibbutz
   - Ⓒ persuade people to live on a kibbutz
   - Ⓓ tell a made-up story about a child on a kibbutz

3. At the end of the passage, the author gives information about life on a kibbutz today to show that _____.
   - Ⓐ all the people still do everything together
   - Ⓑ everyone who lives on a kibbutz is happy
   - Ⓒ things have changed a lot since the first kibbutz
   - Ⓓ the people of Israel are very friendly

4. How does the author of this passage seem to feel about having the children on a kibbutz sleep together in children's houses? Give a detail from the passage to support your answer.
   _____
   _____

5. Write a clue from the passage that suggests that the author thinks that the old way of life on a kibbutz was better than the new way.
   _____
   _____

Name _____  Date _____

Directions: Read the passage. Then use the information from the passage to answer questions 1–5.

# The Mystery of Stonehenge

Stonehenge is one of England's great mysteries. It is a circle of huge stones on an empty plain. The place is quite remarkable. You can see the stones from miles away. They rise high into the sky.

These giant stones are very heavy. They weigh up to 50 tons each. No one knows how the stones were moved to the site. A study shows it would have taken 600 people to move one stone.

Scientists have studied the stones closely. They found that the construction was done in three stages. The first stage went from around 2,950 to 2,900 B.C.E. Builders dug large ditches in a circle. A huge stone called the heel stone was placed at the entrance.

The second stage went from 2,900 to 2,400 B.C.E. Builders dug an inner ditch. The third stage went from 2,550 to 1,600 B.C.E. Builders placed two circles of stones inside the ditch circles. In the center, they placed another stone. This is called the altar stone.

Why was Stonehenge built? Some people think it was used to study the sun, moon, and stars. The sun shines through some of the stones in an unusual way at different times of the year, especially in spring and fall when the seasons change. Others feel that the site had religious uses. It may have been used in burial rites.

Stonehenge may have been used for both astronomy and religion. Ancient people worshipped the sun and moon. They had festivals when the seasons changed. Stonehenge could have been a place to worship the skies and the changing of the seasons.

Name _____ Date _____

1. **Which sentence from the passage states a fact about Stonehenge?**
   - Ⓐ They weigh up to 50 tons each.
   - Ⓑ The place is quite remarkable.
   - Ⓒ It may have been used in burial rites.
   - Ⓓ Stonehenge is one of England's great mysteries.

2. **What evidence supports the fact that Stonehenge was built in three stages?**
   - Ⓐ It would have taken 600 people to move one stone.
   - Ⓑ It has two circles of stones.
   - Ⓒ The sun shines through the stones when the seasons change.
   - Ⓓ Scientists have studied Stonehenge closely.

3. **Which of these is an opinion about Stonehenge?**
   - Ⓐ It is a circle of stones on an empty plain.
   - Ⓑ Stonehenge is quite a remarkable place.
   - Ⓒ It would have taken 600 people to move one stone.
   - Ⓓ The first stage of building went from 2,950 to 2,900 B.C.E.

4. **Write a sentence from the passage that states a fact. Tell how you know it is a fact.**

   _____

   _____

5. **What information supports the opinion that Stonehenge might have been used both for religious and astronomical purposes?**

   _____

   _____

Name _____ Date _____

Directions: Read the passage. Then use the information from the passage to answer questions 1–5.

# The Sox and the Bambino

In 1918, the Boston Red Sox won the World Series by beating the Chicago Cubs. One of their stars that year was a young player named Babe Ruth, also known as "The Babe" or "The Bambino." By any name, he was the greatest baseball player of all time.

In 1920, the owner of the Red Sox traded Babe Ruth to the New York Yankees for $100,000. It was the worst trade ever made. The Yankees had never won a World Series, but with Babe Ruth they began winning. Over the next 83 years, they won 26 World Series.

During that time, the Red Sox never won again, and some Sox fans blamed it on the trade. They believed the Babe had put some kind of hex on them. They called it "The Curse of the Bambino."

Of course, nobody really believes in curses. Still, bad things seemed to happen to the Sox at the worst times. Take the 1946 World Series, which came down to the last game. A player on the St. Louis team was coming home with the winning run. The Red Sox second baseman held the ball and the Sox lost. It was not fair that St. Louis won that game.

The same kind of disaster happened in the 1986 World Series against the New York Mets. The Sox were winning, and the game was down to the last out. The ball rolled down to the Red Sox first baseman and went between his legs. The Sox lost again. It was the worst day in the history of baseball.

It looked to be the same story in 2004 when the Sox were playing the Yankees in the playoffs. The Yankees won the first three games, and they were ahead in the fourth game. Many fans may have thought the series was over, but then a wonderful thing happened. The Red Sox tied the game and went on to win in the twelfth inning.

The Red Sox did not lose again that fall. After 86 years, they finally won the World Series, and the "Curse of the Bambino" was put to rest.

Name _____  Date _____

1. **Which sentence gives an opinion about Babe Ruth?**
   - Ⓐ He was also known as "The Babe" or "The Bambino."
   - Ⓑ The owner of the Red Sox traded Babe Ruth to the New York Yankees.
   - Ⓒ With Babe Ruth, the Yankees began winning.
   - Ⓓ By any name, he was the greatest baseball player of all time.

2. **Which sentence from the passage states a fact?**
   - Ⓐ It was not fair that St. Louis won that game.
   - Ⓑ The "Curse of the Bambino" was put to rest.
   - Ⓒ Over the next 83 years, they won 26 World Series.
   - Ⓓ It was the worst day in the history of baseball.

3. **Which sentence from the passage expresses an opinion?**
   - Ⓐ Of course, nobody really believes in curses.
   - Ⓑ Take the 1946 World Series, which came down to the last game.
   - Ⓒ The ball rolled down to the Red Sox first baseman and went between his legs.
   - Ⓓ The Red Sox did not lose again that fall.

4. **The passage says, "Many fans may have thought the series was over, but then a wonderful thing happened." Does this sentence state a fact or an opinion? Tell how you know.**

   _____
   _____

5. **Write a sentence from the passage and tell whether it states a fact or an opinion.**

   _____
   _____

# Sailing to California

In the 1850s, the trip west to California was long and hard. It could take months. People traveled in heavy covered wagons. They carried food for the long trip as well as clothes and other supplies. Most of the wagons were pulled by oxen, horses, or mules, but the animals had trouble pulling the wagons uphill and downhill. The animals got very tired, and some even died on the trip.

Zeb Thomas thought long and hard about this problem. Thomas wanted to find a way to travel across the prairie without using animals. He knew the prairies were flat and windy. He wanted to build a special wagon with a sail so the wind would push it along the ground. Thomas hoped that his idea would work and would make him rich.

Zeb Thomas became known as "Windwagon" Thomas. He found several investors who gave him money to help him build his wagon. These people hoped the windwagon would make them rich, too.

Windwagon Thomas got his wagon ready for its first trip. It was twenty-five feet long and seven feet wide with wheels over ten feet high. In the center of the wagon was a seven-foot mast with a sail.

People crowded around to watch the wagon's first trip. The sail picked up the wind, and the wagon started to roll. The windwagon worked! When the wind grew stronger, the wagon went faster. Then the trail dipped down the side of a hill. The wagon, moving at a very high speed, smashed into the side of the hill. It was crushed.

Thomas crawled out of the wreck. He wasn't hurt, but his investors were so angry that they ran him out of town. That was the last time anyone tried to build a windwagon.

Name _____ Date_____

1. Why was the trip to California so difficult for oxen, horses, and mules?
   Ⓐ They were not fed properly.
   Ⓑ Most of the land was flat.
   Ⓒ They had to pull heavy wagons.
   Ⓓ The wind blew all the time.

2. Why did Windwagon Thomas want his wagon to work?
   Ⓐ He wanted to be famous.
   Ⓑ He thought it would make him rich.
   Ⓒ He had made a bet with someone about it.
   Ⓓ It was his greatest dream.

3. What was the result of the windwagon's first trip?
   Ⓐ The wagon worked beautifully.
   Ⓑ The animals got tired.
   Ⓒ The investors gave Thomas money.
   Ⓓ The wagon crashed.

4. What caused the wagon to crash?
   _____
   _____

5. How did the windwagon's crash affect the investors? Tell what they did.
   _____
   _____

Name _____ Date _____

Directions: Read the passage. Then use the information from the passage to answer questions 1–5.

# Saving Joseph

On July 6, 1885, Joseph Meister was only nine years old. But his chances of reaching ten were almost zero. Joseph had been bitten by a mad dog that had rabies. Then and now, rabies could kill you.

Joseph's family lived in a French village. His mother took him to the city of Paris to see a scientist named Louis Pasteur. Pasteur had just found a way to cure rabies, or so he thought. His new cure had not been tested yet.

Pasteur knew that Joseph could not wait, but Pasteur was worried. He was not a doctor. If his "cure" killed the boy, he could go to jail.

Later, people asked why Pasteur risked everything for a sick little boy. Louis Pasteur had been fighting disease his whole life. He thought most diseases were caused by germs. Germs are small, unseen creatures. They live in the air and water. They grow inside and outside the body. Pasteur had found cures for some diseases. His ideas led to many other cures.

Pasteur won many prizes, but he also knew great sadness. Three of his five children had died of disease. Some people think that is what pushed him to fight illnesses. When Pasteur saw Joseph, maybe he remembered his own dying children.

Pasteur decided to risk everything. He gave his new cure to Joseph Meister, and the boy lived.

When Pasteur died ten years later, his body was placed in the Pasteur Institute in Paris. Later, Joseph Meister worked as the caretaker there. Meister died in 1940 defending the Institute against the German army. Joseph was sixty-four. He had lived a full life, thanks to Louis Pasteur.

Name _____  Date _____

1. **What caused Joseph Meister to get sick in 1885?**
   - Ⓐ He got bit by a dog with rabies.
   - Ⓑ He visited Paris for the first time.
   - Ⓒ Pasteur gave him some medicine.
   - Ⓓ His chances of reaching ten were almost zero.

2. **Joseph's mother took him to Paris because she _____.**
   - Ⓐ knew he had never seen Paris before
   - Ⓑ thought Pasteur should go to jail
   - Ⓒ wanted Louis Pasteur to treat him
   - Ⓓ was going to work at the Pasteur Institute

3. **Why was Pasteur worried about helping Joseph?**
   - Ⓐ His cure was not working on children.
   - Ⓑ The boy was too young.
   - Ⓒ The boy's chances of reaching ten were almost zero.
   - Ⓓ He could go to jail if the boy died.

4. **What is the most likely reason why Pasteur decided to treat Joseph?**

   _____
   _____

5. **What effect did Pasteur's treatment have on Joseph?**

   _____
   _____

Name _____ Date _____

Directions: Read the passage. Then use the information from the passage to answer questions 1–5.

# The Lost Colony

In the 1600s, many people from England sailed to America. They wanted to build new towns and start new lives. The first permanent English settlement was Jamestown. It was founded in Virginia in 1607. The Pilgrims founded Plymouth in 1620. There was another colony before either of these two, but it disappeared.

In 1585, Sir Walter Raleigh sent 108 men to America. They landed on Roanoke Island. That is off the coast of what is now North Carolina. A year later they were starving. So they returned to England.

In 1587, Raleigh sent another group of settlers to Roanoke. There were 117 men, women, and children. The leader was a man named John White. His daughter was Eleanor Dare. She had a baby soon after the group arrived. The baby was named Virginia Dare. She was the first English child born in America.

After only a week at Roanoke, John White sailed back to England. He had to get more tools and supplies. But England went to war with Spain soon after that. So White stayed in England for almost three years.

When John White finally returned to Roanoke in 1590, the people were gone. The only clue left behind was the word *Croatoan*. It was carved into a post. Croatoan was the name of a nearby island. So White thought the people had moved to a better place. However, none of the colonists was ever seen again. To this day, no one knows what happened to them.

Name _____ Date_____

1. What is this passage mostly about?
   - Ⓐ the colony of Jamestown, Virginia
   - Ⓑ the birth of a child named Virginia Dare
   - Ⓒ a colony in America that disappeared
   - Ⓓ the war between England and Spain

2. According to the passage, where was the first English settlement in America?
   - Ⓐ Jamestown
   - Ⓑ Croatoan
   - Ⓒ Plymouth
   - Ⓓ Roanoke Island

3. In one sentence, write the main idea of the third paragraph in your own words.

   _____
   _____

4. Which detail supports the idea that the people of the Roanoke colony had planned to move to another place?
   - Ⓐ John White remained in England.
   - Ⓑ The word *Croatoan* was carved into a post.
   - Ⓒ England went to war with Spain.
   - Ⓓ The first English child was born at Roanoke.

5. Write a detail from the passage supporting the idea that John White stayed in England too long before he returned to Roanoke.

   _____
   _____

©2015 Benchmark Education Company, LLC          Comprehension Strategy Assessment • Grade 4   71

Name _____ Date _____

Directions: *Read the passage. Then use the information from the passage to answer questions 1–5.*

# A New Kind of Studio

You probably have heard of the movie *Toy Story*, and maybe you have seen it. Maybe you have also seen *Toy Story 2* and *3*. How about *Cars*, *WALL-E*, or *Up*? These cartoon movies were all made at the same place—a studio called Pixar.

In 1979, George Lucas had a wish. He is the man who created the Star Wars movies. He and his crew wanted to come up with a brand-new way to make cartoon movies. Lucas started a company to make his wish come true.

In those days, it took years to make a cartoon movie. People had to make one drawing at a time. Each drawing might show a creature or a character doing something, such as taking a step.

It took about twenty-four of these pictures to make one second in a cartoon. Movies often last from ninety minutes to more than two hours. That's over one hundred thousand drawings per movie! No wonder it took forever to make one.

Lucas's crew came up with ways to create the drawings for cartoons on computers. It took them until 1984 to finish their first short movie. Not long after that, Steve Jobs, who had helped start Apple computers, bought the company from Lucas and named it Pixar. Pixar got better and better at using computers to make the drawings, and the drawings look so real. Just the balloons in *Up*, for example, are amazing to watch.

When *Toy Story* came out in 1995, it didn't look like any movie ever made. Kids and grown-ups loved it, and many watched it again and again. Pixar's first six movies made almost three billion dollars. Many Pixar movies Pixar movies have won awards for best animated film of the year. It's no wonder that cartoon-lovers look forward to each new movie from the studio.

Name _____ Date _____

1. Which would be another good title for this passage?
   Ⓐ "Old-Fashioned Cartoons"
   Ⓑ "The Story of *Toy Story*"
   Ⓒ "A Company Called Pixar"
   Ⓓ "Kids and Grown-Ups"

2. Which sentence from the passage tells the main idea of the third paragraph?
   Ⓐ In those days, it took years to make one cartoon.
   Ⓑ People had to make one drawing at a time.
   Ⓒ Each drawing might show a creature or a character doing something, such as taking a step.
   Ⓓ It took about twenty-four of these pictures to make one second in a cartoon.

3. What is the main idea of the fifth paragraph?
   Ⓐ The company was named Pixar.
   Ⓑ Pixar uses computers to improve how cartoons are made.
   Ⓒ The computer drawings look real.
   Ⓓ The balloons in *Up* are amazing.

4. Write a detail from the passage supporting the idea that George Lucas created a new kind of studio to make movies.

   _____
   _____

5. Write a detail from the passage supporting the idea that Pixar has been very successful so far.

   _____
   _____

Name _____ Date _____

Directions: Read the passage. Then use the information from the passage to answer questions 1–5.

# Sail Away

Did you know that you can use sticks and leaves to build sailboats and villages? Here's how.

> **Things You Will Need:**
> - many small sticks less than 8 inches long
> - leaves of different shapes and sizes
> - string
> - glue

**Step 1:** To make a sailboat, choose ten sticks of the same length and pull off any leaves attached to the sticks.

**Step 2:** Place six to eight sticks side by side. Glue the sticks together. When the glue is dry, tie the sticks at both ends with string, making sure the sticks stay flat. This will make the bottom of your sailboat.

**Step 3:** Choose one stick and stand it up between two sticks in the middle of your boat. Choose a leaf you can use as a sail for your boat, and attach the sail with glue.

**Step 4:** When the glue is dry, place your finished boat in a stream or brook and let it sail. Watch how the wind pushes the boat along swiftly.

**Step 5:** With other sticks, you can build a village on the banks of the stream or brook. Sticks of the same length can be tied together to form the walls of houses, and leaves or sticks can be used to make roofs for the houses.

Name _____ Date_____

1. After you gather the things you need, what is the first step in this project?

   _____
   _____

2. What should you do next after you finish the bottom of your boat?
   - Ⓐ Place six to eight sticks of the same length side by side.
   - Ⓑ See if the sailboat sails in the wind.
   - Ⓒ Make roofs for stick houses with leaves.
   - Ⓓ Stand a stick up in the middle of the boat bottom.

3. What are you making in Step 3 of this passage?
   - Ⓐ a village
   - Ⓑ a sail
   - Ⓒ a bridge
   - Ⓓ the bottom of a boat

4. What could you do when the sailboat is finished and the glue has dried?

   _____
   _____

5. Which step tells you how to build a stick village?
   - Ⓐ Step 2
   - Ⓑ Step 3
   - Ⓒ Step 4
   - Ⓓ Step 5

# A Long Journey

The monarch butterflies of North America do something no other butterflies do. When fall comes, they leave their homes in the northern United States and Canada. They travel 3,000 miles to spend the winter in California or Mexico. They travel north again in the spring.

Monarch butterfly eggs hatch in the late summer. First, the butterflies gain energy by drinking nectar from flowers. Then they begin the trip south. The butterflies can fly at speeds of up to twelve miles an hour. They also glide on the air to save energy.

Monarch butterflies travel in large groups. They face many dangers during the journey. Storms can push them off course or kill them. Many die when they fly into moving trucks and cars. Others are eaten by birds. Some just get too tired to finish the trip. Still, a large number of butterflies finish the trip. In one part of Mexico, up to 300 million monarchs spend the winter.

In late February, the butterflies begin to move north again. They lay eggs along the way. New butterflies hatch and continue the trip. Finally, these new butterflies reach their summer homes.

Scientists wonder how monarch butterflies know where to go in the fall and spring. No butterfly ever lives long enough to make the trip more than once. Yet they always return to the same places. What tells them where to go? Scientists hope to learn the answer to this puzzle someday.

Name _____ Date_____

1. What do monarch butterflies do first to get ready for their trip south?
   - Ⓐ  They rest for the winter.
   - Ⓑ  They lay eggs.
   - Ⓒ  They fly on air currents.
   - Ⓓ  They drink nectar for energy.

2. What happens last on the trip north?
   - Ⓐ  The monarchs are eaten by birds.
   - Ⓑ  The monarchs reach their summer homes.
   - Ⓒ  The monarchs lay eggs.
   - Ⓓ  The monarchs drink nectar.

3. What do these butterflies do when fall comes?
   - Ⓐ  They begin to fly south.
   - Ⓑ  They lay eggs.
   - Ⓒ  They begin to fly north.
   - Ⓓ  They arrive at their summer homes.

4. According to the passage, what happens in late February?
   _____
   _____

5. Write two sentences using signal words to describe what the butterflies do after they begin their trip north.
   _____
   _____

©2015 Benchmark Education Company, LLC

Name _____ Date _____

Directions: Read the passage. Then use the information from the passage to answer questions 1–5.

# Camels of the Plant World

The cactus is the camel of the plant world. Like camels, cactuses (or cacti) live in the desert and can survive a long time on little water. Camels can be "prickly" animals, as cacti are prickly, and they are ugly.

Some people think that cacti are ugly, too, but others keep them in their homes. That is partly because cacti are easy to care for. But they can also be quite beautiful. They have flowers of all shapes and colors. These flowers can be white, red, purple, orange, or copper.

Cacti may be flowery, but they are not wimps like other houseplants. Cacti know how to take care of themselves. Your dog may knock over some plants. Your cat might try to eat others. But if they try anything with a cactus, they'll get a pawful of needles.

The cactus is as American as apple pie. Many kinds of cacti grow only in the United States. But some can be found as far south as Chile. Others grow as far north as Canada. One kind can be found in Africa.

Cacti come in all shapes and sizes. The saguaro cacti found in Arizona, California, and Mexico can grow as tall as fifty feet. In the dark, they look like giant men with their arms held up.

Cacti can look like many things. One kind is like a big pincushion with pins sticking out. The fishhook cactus looks like a pile of fishhooks. Another group of cacti look like hedgehogs, or porcupines, covered with quills. Three kinds of cacti look like prickly pears.

Some cacti are very rare, and scientists worry that they may disappear. It is against the law to collect cacti in the wild. It is also against the law to harm them.

Name _____ Date_____

1. The passage says, "Cacti are not wimps like other houseplants." What does this mean?
   Ⓐ Cacti are not good to eat.
   Ⓑ Cacti are not really houseplants.
   Ⓒ Cacti have beautiful flowers that people like.
   Ⓓ Cacti have needles to protect themselves.

2. According to the passage, "The cactus is as American as apple pie" because _____.
   Ⓐ many cacti grow only in the United States.
   Ⓑ many cacti have the same shape and color as apples
   Ⓒ cacti are sometimes used in pies
   Ⓓ cactus flowers are mostly red, white, and blue

3. The author of this passage compares saguaro cacti to _____.
   Ⓐ trees
   Ⓑ large men
   Ⓒ camels
   Ⓓ pincushions

4. Why does the author of this passage say that the cactus is "the camel of the plant world"?
   _____
   _____

5. Write a sentence from the passage that uses figurative language and tell what is being compared in the sentence.
   _____
   _____

©2015 Benchmark Education Company, LLC       Comprehension Strategy Assessment • Grade 4   79

**Directions:** Read the passage. Then use the information from the passage to answer questions 1–5.

# Aunt Tallulah's Carpet

Mattie and I never knew what to expect when we visited Aunt Tallulah. Sometimes we sat around all afternoon playing gin rummy or checkers. Those days were about as exciting as watching paint dry. But at other times, she told us stories about the old days or showed us some of the things she had collected over the years. Those were our favorite times. Her house was a museum, and she enjoyed giving tours.

One Saturday afternoon, Mattie and I followed Aunt Tallulah up to the attic in her house. She wore a really old costume dress that day. It had huge blue feathers on the back like a peacock. Mattie loved that dress and said she wanted one just like it.

The attic was filled with cobwebs and dust and plenty of spiders. The piles of objects on the floor were like big bugs wrapped in silk webs. Maybe a giant spider was saving them for food to be eaten later.

Aunt Tallulah picked up a rug that was rolled up in the corner of the attic. She took one end of the carpet. Then she snapped it in the air like a bullwhip. Suddenly, the colors of the carpet came alive, and it wriggled like a snake. The deep reds and blues sparkled like jewels. When she let go of the carpet, it hovered over the floor and made a whirring sound like a helicopter ready to take off!

"Wow!" said Mattie at the same time as I gasped. We had seen some cool things at Aunt Tallulah's house before, but we had never seen anything like this.

Name _____ Date _____

1. The passage says, "Those days were about as exciting as watching paint dry." What does this sentence mean?
   - Ⓐ Those days were exciting because we painted.
   - Ⓑ Watching and painting made those days exciting.
   - Ⓒ Those days were slow and boring.
   - Ⓓ When we watched the paint, it did not dry.

2. The passage says, "Her house was a museum." What does this sentence mean?
   - Ⓐ There were many interesting things to see in her house.
   - Ⓑ People who went to her house had to pay admission.
   - Ⓒ Her house was kept open for people to see.
   - Ⓓ Everything in the house looked the same as it did hundreds of years ago.

3. In this passage, the author compares Aunt Tallulah's dress to a _____.
   - Ⓐ spider
   - Ⓑ carpet
   - Ⓒ snake
   - Ⓓ peacock

4. In the third paragraph, what kind of figurative language does the author use to describe the objects in the attic?
   _____
   _____

5. Write a sentence from the passage that uses figurative language and tell what is being compared in the sentence.
   _____
   _____

©2015 Benchmark Education Company, LLC    Comprehension Strategy Assessment • Grade 4

## Ongoing Comprehension Strategy Assessment • 23

Name _____  Date _____

Directions: Read the passage. Then use the information from the passage to answer questions 1–5.

# The Voice of History

*A TV newsperson is speaking to the viewing audience from behind a desk. It is the beginning of the nightly news.*

**ELISE:** Good evening from Washington, D.C. Our reporter, Melvin James, is on the steps of the Lincoln Memorial. He has some late-breaking news.

**MELVIN:** Hello, Elise. I'm talking with Denise Crowley. Ms. Crowley, please tell our viewers what you heard a while ago.

**DENISE:** *(looking scared but excited)* I'm not sure anyone will believe me, but the statue of Lincoln spoke to me.

**MELVIN:** What did it say?

**LINCOLN'S STATUE:** *(loud voice)* I said, "Four score and seven years ago."

**MELVIN AND DENISE:** *(looking up at the statue)* President Lincoln!

**ELISE:** *(in a voice shaky and low)* Incredible! President Lincoln, welcome to our news show. Please tell us how it is that we are hearing your voice. I mean *(voice lowers and slows)* you died in 1865. You're a statue.

**LINCOLN'S STATUE:** I was assassinated at the end of the Civil War—that's true. But my ideas live on. That's what history is all about. I want all Americans to know that history is real people and real actions.

**ELISE:** *(looking at the camera)* Thank you, Mr. President. This has been a very special news event, indeed.

Name _____ Date_____

1. When does this play take place?
   Ⓐ during the Civil War
   Ⓑ four score and seven (87) years ago
   Ⓒ in 1865
   Ⓓ in the present

2. Write two details from the passage that give clues to when the play takes place.
   _____
   _____

3. Why is Melvin at the Lincoln Memorial?
   Ⓐ He is going to a rally.
   Ⓑ A protest will soon take place there.
   Ⓒ The statue of Lincoln has been speaking.
   Ⓓ He is looking for Ms. Crowley.

4. From what Denise says and how she acts when she is first interviewed by Melvin, you can tell that she is _____.
   Ⓐ nervous and excited
   Ⓑ smart and watchful
   Ⓒ serious and plain
   Ⓓ calm and quiet

5. How does Elise feel when she first hears the voice of the statue? Explain why you think so.
   _____
   _____

Name _____ Date _____

Directions: Read the passage. Then use the information from the passage to answer questions 1–5.

# Mapping the Pacific

In the mid-1700s, Europeans knew very little about the Pacific Ocean. Almost no one had been there. They thought there might be a continent in the South Pacific. If there were, England wanted it. But who would make such a long, hard trip to find out?

Captain James Cook was just the man. His dream was to travel farther than any man had ever been.

Captain Cook came from a poor family. He was a smart and curious boy who learned quickly. When he started working on ships, his interest in math helped him become a great navigator. Then he joined the British Navy and became a maker of maps. His maps of Canada's St. Lawrence River were used into the early 1900s.

From 1768 to 1779, Captain Cook sailed around the world three times for England. Each trip took three or four years. He explored New Zealand and Australia. He found many islands, such as Hawaii. Scientists then thought there might be land at the South Pole. He sailed close to Antarctica three times but was too far away to see it. Ice always forced him to turn back. Still, he sailed farther south than any other explorer.

Captain Cook also made history by keeping his men alive. At the time, sailors ate mostly salted meat and bread crawling with bugs. No wonder so many of them became ill and often died! He gave his men fresh fruit and vegetables. This kept them from getting sick on long ocean trips.

The great Captain James Cook did travel farther than any man had ever been. He went as far as it was possible to go.

Name _____ Date_____

1. From the passage, what can you infer about Captain Cook?
   - Ⓐ He was very brave.
   - Ⓑ He was a fool to take such risks.
   - Ⓒ He was spoiled as a child.
   - Ⓓ He was afraid of ice.

2. You can infer from the passage that a navigator is a person who _____.
   - Ⓐ travels a lot
   - Ⓑ comes from a poor family
   - Ⓒ learns quickly
   - Ⓓ guides a ship from place to place

3. From the information in this passage, what can you infer about Cook's maps of Canada?
   - Ⓐ There was no money to make new maps.
   - Ⓑ His maps were quite accurate.
   - Ⓒ Not many ship captains used his maps.
   - Ⓓ Cook was a skilled artist.

4. Why didn't most sailors in the 1700s eat more fruits and vegetables?
   _____
   _____

5. Write one or two clues from the passage suggesting that most people of the 1700s did not know much about the rest of the world.
   _____
   _____

Name _____ Date _____

Directions: Read the passage. Then use the information from the passage to answer questions 1–5.

# Benjamin Banneker

Benjamin Banneker was born in 1731. At that time, America still belonged to England. Most African Americans were slaves then. But Benjamin was a free black man. His family farmed land in Maryland.

Ben was always a smart young man. He loved numbers. He counted everything in sight. He never tired of learning.

In 1771, the Ellicotts moved next door to the Banneker farm. George Ellicott became an important friend to Ben. Ellicott shared his telescope with Ben and taught him astronomy, the study of the stars and planets. He also taught Ben how to survey land and make maps. With Ellicott's telescope, Ben studied the night sky. He also studied the movements of the sun and moon.

In 1791, a cousin of George Ellicott offered a job to Banneker. He asked Ben to help make plans for the new capital of the United States in Washington, D.C. Ben's job was to mark a ten-mile square for the new city. To do this, he used his knowledge of the sun and stars and his surveying skills. He also used a special clock.

When Ben finished his work, he returned to his farm and his own projects. One of these was his almanac, a book that gave information about weather and the seasons. Banneker continued to study the stars and survey the land until his death in 1806.

Name _____  Date _____

1. Which detail from the passage supports the judgment that part of Benjamin Banneker's success came from his friendship with George Ellicott?
   - Ⓐ The Ellicotts lived next door to the Banneker farm.
   - Ⓑ Ellicott became an important friend to Ben.
   - Ⓒ Ben was a free black man who lived in Maryland.
   - Ⓓ Ben returned to his farm and his own projects.

2. What were the most important things that Benjamin Banneker learned from George Ellicott?

   _____

   _____

3. Why was Benjamin Banneker the right person to do the job of marking the area that would become the new United States capital?

   _____

   _____

4. What part of Benjamin Banneker's work was probably most important to farmers?
   - Ⓐ his almanac
   - Ⓑ his plans for Washington, D.C.
   - Ⓒ his love of numbers
   - Ⓓ his studies of the night sky

5. Which detail from the passage best supports the judgment that Benjamin Banneker was a skilled scientist?
   - Ⓐ He always loved numbers and counted everything in sight.
   - Ⓑ He shared George Ellicott's telescope.
   - Ⓒ He used his knowledge of the sun and stars to plan a new city.
   - Ⓓ He returned to his farm and his own projects.

Name _____ Date _____

Directions: Read the passage. Then use the information from the passage to answer questions 1–5.

# A Life in Pictures

Margaret Bourke-White was a photojournalist. She took pictures for newspapers, magazines, and books. Her pictures show a great understanding of people. They also show her amazing bravery.

Bourke-White started taking pictures in college. Later, she began to do it for a living. Most women did not work in those days, but that did not stop her. At first she took pictures of buildings. Then a man named Henry Luce asked her to work for him. Luce started *Life* magazine. Bourke-White took the first cover picture for *Life*.

Margaret Bourke-White took many pictures of people. They show people's pain, happiness, fear, and anger. These pictures show her deep understanding of human emotions.

Someone asked Bourke-White what she thought was her best picture. She said it was one she took during the Korean War. It showed a meeting between a soldier and his mother. The mother thought her son had been killed. The picture shows the joy she felt at seeing him alive.

Sometimes Bourke-White's work was dangerous. She took many pictures during wars. Some of them show bombs falling around her. Once her ship was hit by a torpedo. She was left for days on an island in the Arctic. One of her planes crashed, too. But she never gave up. She thought danger was just part of her job.

Margaret Bourke-White died in 1971. Her pictures live on, though. They tell us about events and people. They also show Margaret Bourke-White's great skill and understanding.

Name _____  Date _____

1. What judgment does the author express in the first paragraph about Margaret Bourke-White's photographs?
    Ⓐ  They show many beautiful, natural sites.
    Ⓑ  They show terrible storms.
    Ⓒ  They show a great understanding of people.
    Ⓓ  They help people understand animals.

2. What evidence supports the author's judgment of Margaret Bourke-White?
    Ⓐ  Her photos show the horrors of war.
    Ⓑ  Her photos show beautiful models and actors.
    Ⓒ  Her photos show scary times and places.
    Ⓓ  Her photos show people's feelings and emotions.

3. What judgment did Margaret Bourke-White make about one picture she took during the Korean War?
    Ⓐ  It is a very sad picture.
    Ⓑ  It shows a soldier and his mother.
    Ⓒ  It is her best picture.
    Ⓓ  It will help people understand war.

4. What was probably the bravest thing Margaret Bourke-White did?
   _____
   _____

5. Write two details from the passage to support the judgment that Margaret Bourke-White's job was often dangerous.
   _____
   _____

# Ongoing Comprehension Strategy Assessment • 27

Name _____  Date _____

Directions: Read the passage. Then use the information from the passage to answer questions 1–5.

# A Backward Look

Ralph felt much better after his nap. He reached for the plastic container his mother had filled with old family photographs. He would organize and then paste them into an album now, knowing that his mother would not let him stay home from school another day.

The first photograph he picked up showed a man standing in front of a small wooden cabin. To the right of the man stood a horse and a wagon filled with bales of hay. The man strongly resembled Ralph's grandfather and his mother.

Suddenly, the room began to spin and Ralph fell back on his pillow. When the spinning stopped, Ralph was standing outside.

"That hay is for market, young man. Saddle up and let's get going," the man said to Ralph.

Ralph was wearing heavy cotton pants, a big felt hat, and a pair of leather boots he had never seen before. But when he spoke, he sounded exactly like himself: Ralph Finks.

"Sir, I, uh—" Ralph stammered.

"You did a fine job hitching up the wagon, son," said the man as he gave Ralph a friendly slap on the back. "Now let's say good-bye and get on the trail. It's market day."

A woman stepped out of the cabin wearing a long dress with a white cotton apron over it. She held up a bag tied with string and called, "Don't forget your biscuits!"

Ralph just stood by the wagon staring at the woman, who smiled just like his aunt May as she said, "Come and get your biscuits and bacon, Jamie Kleinholz!"

"Kleinholz!" Ralph gasped. "That's Grandma and Grandpa's last name!"

Name _____  Date _____

1. In the story, what will the young man called Jamie probably do next?
   - Ⓐ He will take a nap.
   - Ⓑ He will take the hay to market.
   - Ⓒ He will bake some biscuits.
   - Ⓓ He will go back to school.

2. In his real life, what did Ralph probably do the next day?
   - Ⓐ He made a new photo album.
   - Ⓑ He stayed with Jamie Kleinholz.
   - Ⓒ He went back to school.
   - Ⓓ He drove the wagon to the market.

3. Who is the woman with the bag of biscuits? Explain how you know.

   _____

   _____

4. If the story continued, what would Ralph most likely say to the woman with the biscuits?

   _____

   _____

5. Which prediction best explains how Ralph will get back to his own home?
   - Ⓐ He will wake up.
   - Ⓑ He will ride a horse.
   - Ⓒ He will get on an airplane.
   - Ⓓ He will walk a long way.

# Sally Ride, Scientist and Space Explorer

Have you ever wanted to spend a week in a small room with four other people? That's how it is in a space shuttle. Flying in a tiny spaceship isn't easy, and only the best are chosen for it. Sally Ride was one of them. She was the first U.S. woman in space.

Once, Sally wanted to be a tennis player. Then she got interested in science. She worked hard to become a scientist. In 1978, she was chosen from 8,000 people to be an astronaut. Astronauts spend years training before they go into space. They have to be able to handle anything that happens. From flying jets to fixing radios, she did it all. Astronauts also have special jobs. One of her jobs was running a robot arm she had helped to make.

In June 1983, Dr. Ride got to put all her training to work. She and four other astronauts took off and spent a week in the space shuttle *Challenger*. In her book *To Space and Back*, she described what it was like to float hundreds of miles above Earth. The next year she flew on the *Challenger* again. She was training for a third trip when the *Challenger* blew up. Everyone on board that day was killed.

After retiring as an astronaut, Dr. Ride taught science at the University of California. She also helped girls who wanted to become scientists. She set up science programs for them and told them to work hard at science and math.

Sally Ride knew what it was like to have big dreams. She said that one of her goals was "to make science and engineering cool again." When she died in 2012, President Obama called her "a national hero and a powerful role model."

Name _____ Date _____

1. You can guess that as a girl, Sally Ride probably was _____.
   - Ⓐ not very interested in school
   - Ⓑ good at sports
   - Ⓒ the friendliest person in her class
   - Ⓓ afraid of flying

2. Which of these would Sally Ride most likely have said to a girl who wanted to be a scientist?
   - Ⓐ "You should try playing tennis."
   - Ⓑ "Not many girls get to be astronauts."
   - Ⓒ "You can do whatever you set your mind to."
   - Ⓓ "If you can't be a scientist, try tennis."

3. If you looked through Sally Ride's book, *To Space and Back*, you would most likely see pictures of _____.
   - Ⓐ how Earth looks from space
   - Ⓑ Sally Ride playing tennis
   - Ⓒ where the University of California is located
   - Ⓓ Sally Ride's parents

4. If Sally Ride had not become an astronaut, what would she probably have done?

   _____

5. Sally Ride was the first U.S. woman in space. How did her experiences probably affect the chances of other women becoming astronauts?

   _____

   _____

Name _____ Date _____

Directions: Read the passage. Then use the information from the passage to answer questions 1–5.

# Calendars

The Western calendar that we use today began in Rome more than 2,000 years ago.

**The Western Calendar**

Around 45 B.C.E., Julius Caesar was the ruler of Rome. He called for a new calendar. It was called the Julian calendar. It was based on the lunar cycle, or the time it takes the moon to orbit Earth. It is also the time it takes the moon to go from a new moon to a full moon and back to a new moon again. That is about 29½ days. A year in the Julian calendar measures the days by one orbit of Earth around the sun. That is about 365 days.

The Julian calendar was fairly accurate. But it lost one day every 128 years. By 1582, it was ten days off. Pope Gregory XIII corrected it by adding an extra day to the month of February every four years. This is what we call a "leap year." This new system was called the Gregorian calendar.

**Other Calendars**

Different calendars are used by people around the world. They include the Chinese, Islamic, and Hebrew calendars. All three are based on lunar cycles.

The Chinese calendar has 12 or 13 months each year. The calendar goes for 60 years. Then it begins again.

The Islamic, or Muslim, calendar goes for three years and then begins again. It has 12 months. Each month has either 29 or 30 days.

The Hebrew calendar has 12 months each year. Each month has 29 or 30 days. In leap years, an extra month of 29 days is added.

Name _____ Date_____

1. The first two paragraphs of this passage tell mostly about _____.
   - Ⓐ how Earth travels around the sun
   - Ⓑ why Julius Caesar was the ruler of Rome
   - Ⓒ how the Julian calendar came to be
   - Ⓓ what the moon looks like

2. Write one or two sentences summarizing the information in the first part of the passage, "The Western Calendar."

   _____

   _____

3. The second part of the passage, "Other Calendars," tells mostly about _____.
   - Ⓐ Pope Gregory XIII
   - Ⓑ holidays in the Chinese calendar
   - Ⓒ Hebrew numbers
   - Ⓓ examples of other calendars

4. Which is the best description of how the Islamic calendar works?
   - Ⓐ It is a lunar calendar with 12 months in a year and 29 or 30 days in each month.
   - Ⓑ It is sometimes called the Muslim calendar, and it is based on lunar cycles.
   - Ⓒ It is similar to the Chinese and Hebrew calendars in that they are all lunar calendars.
   - Ⓓ It is a three-year calendar with 29 or 30 days in each month.

5. Read the sentence from the passage. Write a paraphrase of this sentence in your own words.

   "It is also the time it takes the moon to go from a new moon to a full moon and back to a new moon again."

   _____

   _____

©2015 Benchmark Education Company, LLC

Name _____ Date _____

Directions: Read the passage. Then use the information from the passage to answer questions 1–5.

# Modern Ranching

In some ways, ranching is the same as it was years ago. Cattle ranchers still ride horses and round up cattle. Many ranchers still use a rope to catch stray cows or calves. But during the past 150 years, ranching has changed a great deal.

One of the biggest changes is that ranchers now drive trucks. For some ranchers, the pickup truck has replaced the horse. Some ranchers even fly planes to find and move cattle. This can be useful when a ranch is very large.

Another new thing in ranching is the Internet. Computers are now a part of ranching. Ranchers can find out about different breeds, or types, of cows. They can also find good deals on feed and the best prices for their beef.

There are Web sites on the Internet with information for ranchers. Groups post facts about the many different topics that ranchers discuss with one another.

Transportation is another big change in ranching. Ranchers no longer have to drive their cattle to market. Now trucks drive right to the ranch where the cowhands load the cattle to be taken away.

These are only some of the ways that ranching has changed. In the old days of cattle drives, cowhands only rode horses. They did everything by hand, and the work was very hard. Today the work is still hard, but ranchers have many high- and low-tech machines to help them.

Name _____ Date _____

1. Which is the best summary of paragraph two?
   Ⓐ Some ranchers now drive trucks instead of riding horses.
   Ⓑ Cattle ranchers still ride horses.
   Ⓒ Ranching today is very different from ranching in the past.
   Ⓓ Ranching is just the same today as it was in the past.

2. Which is the best summary of paragraph three?
   Ⓐ Ranchers may run ads for their beef.
   Ⓑ Ranchers can find feed by using the Internet.
   Ⓒ Ranchers discuss many different topics.
   Ⓓ Ranchers now use computers in many ways.

3. Write a paraphrase of paragraph four in your own words.
   _____
   _____

4. Which sentence best summarizes the last paragraph?
   Ⓐ Ranching has changed in many different ways.
   Ⓑ Ranches are just the same as they were a hundred years ago.
   Ⓒ High-tech machines have changed ranching forever.
   Ⓓ Ranchers still ride horses just as they always have.

5. Summarize the passage in one or two sentences.
   _____
   _____

# What You Hear

Sound is a form of energy that you can hear. Sounds vary in many ways, such as loudness and pitch. A decibel measures how loud a sound is. The graph shows the decibels of some familiar sounds. More than 85 decibels can harm your ears over time. Sounds of more than 100 decibels will cause hearing loss over time. At 120 decibels, sound causes pain.

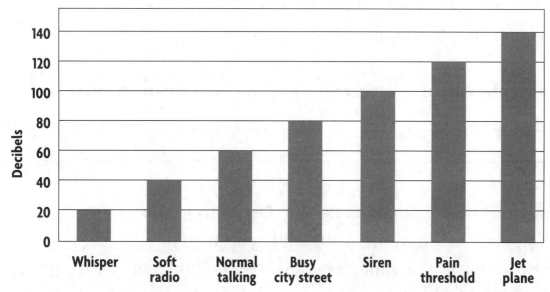

The pitch of a sound varies from low to high. Pitch is measured in hertz (Hz). Can you hear some high-pitched sounds that adults cannot hear? You probably can. As the chart shows, most children hear a greater range of sounds than most adults hear. Some animals can hear high-pitched sounds that people cannot hear.

| Hearing Ranges | |
|---|---|
| Adult Humans | 200–10,000 Hz |
| Children | 20–20,000 Hz |
| Dogs | 15–50,000 Hz |
| Bats | 1,000–120,000 Hz |

Name _____ Date _____

1. Which of these workers would need to wear ear protectors?
   Ⓐ a cook in a restaurant
   Ⓑ a clerk in a department store
   Ⓒ a judge in a courtroom
   Ⓓ a baggage handler at an airport

2. About how many decibels do you hear from city traffic?
   _____

3. Over several years, you would be most likely to hurt your ears if you _____.
   Ⓐ played in a rock-and-roll band
   Ⓑ worked on a farm
   Ⓒ sailed boats on the ocean
   Ⓓ worked at a zoo

4. Which of these can hear sounds at the highest pitch?
   Ⓐ adult human
   Ⓑ bat
   Ⓒ child
   Ⓓ dog

5. According to the graph, what kinds of familiar sounds are the loudest?
   _____
   _____

# The Underground Railroad

Before the Civil War, slavery was legal in some states but not in others. George Washington had slaves in Virginia. In 1786, a group of people called Quakers helped one of his slaves escape. These Quakers were part of a secret system that moved slaves to the North and to Canada. Slavery was illegal in Canada, so the slaves would be free. Later, this system became known as the Underground Railroad. Helping slaves escape was illegal. So it had to be secret, or "underground."

Like a real railroad, this one had stations. These were hiding places where people could rest and eat. Conductors moved the runaways between stations. Harriet Tubman was a conductor. She had escaped from the South. Then she went back. She risked her life many times to bring more slaves to freedom.

Runaways often traveled by night, mostly on foot. They followed the North Star. Often they traveled in winter. Then they could walk across frozen rivers. It could take a year to reach Canada. Some took a path through Ohio. Others went through Maryland or Pennsylvania. Many people took great risks to help slaves escape.

The end of the Civil War brought an end to slavery. But before that, up to 100,000 slaves rode to freedom on the Underground Railroad.

**Slavery in America**

| 1776 | 1784 | 1793 | 1820 | 1830 | 1849 | 1861–1865 |
|------|------|------|------|------|------|-----------|
| Declaration of Independence | Congress keeps slavery legal. | Congress makes it illegal to help slaves escape. | Slavery was made illegal in new Northern states. | Underground Railroad begins. | Harriet Tubman escapes. | Civil War |

Name _____ Date _____

1. Which event happened first?
   Ⓐ  The Civil War started.
   Ⓑ  The Underground Railroad began.
   Ⓒ  Congress voted to keep slavery legal.
   Ⓓ  Harriet Tubman escaped.

2. What did Congress decide in 1793?
   _____
   _____

3. What happened in 1849?
   Ⓐ  The Declaration of Independence was written.
   Ⓑ  The Civil War began.
   Ⓒ  Slavery became illegal.
   Ⓓ  Harriet Tubman escaped from the South.

4. What change took place in 1820?
   _____
   _____

5. When did slavery come to an end in the United States?
   Ⓐ  1830
   Ⓑ  1849
   Ⓒ  1865
   Ⓓ  1870

Name _____ Date _____

Directions: Read the passage. Then use the information from the passage to answer questions 1–5.

# Where Would We Go Without Roads?

Every day we drive on roads without thinking about them. But building a road takes a lot of work.

Why not just clear some land, make it flat, and call it a road? A dirt road is fine if nothing too heavy goes over it and the rain doesn't wash it away, but a road must be strong in order to last.

**Roman Roads**

The first great road builders were the Romans. At one time, the Roman Empire covered most of Western Europe. Roman armies needed wide, straight roads to move from place to place quickly. The Romans built roads three to five feet deep with layers of sand, huge stones, and gravel. Many Roman roads are still used today.

However, even the best roads must be taken care of and repaired. That didn't happen in England. By the early 1800s, the Roman roads in England were in terrible shape. Bad roads made travel hard.

**Modern Roads**

Then Thomas Telford came along. He had built canals and bridges before he turned to roads in 1811. Telford's roads started with a trench. He added a deep layer of heavy rock. On top went 6 inches of gravel. The center was higher than the sides so rain would run off. In some of these roads, tar was used to bind the stones together. This pavement was called **macadam** (named after a Scottish engineer, J.L. McAdam).

Telford's roads were the best of his time. They helped England become a stronger country.

**Not All Roads Are Flat**

For centuries, roads have contributed to the growth of many cultures. The Incas ruled a large part of South America from about 1200 to the 1530s. Since they didn't use the wheel, some of their roads could have steps. One mountain road had 3,000 stone steps. The Inca Empire was united by its many stone roads.

Name _____ Date_____

1. Which part of the passage tells about the Incas?
   - Ⓐ the first paragraph
   - Ⓑ **Roman Roads**
   - Ⓒ **Modern Roads**
   - Ⓓ **Not All Roads Are Flat**

2. Who built roads with steps?
   - Ⓐ the Romans
   - Ⓑ the Incas
   - Ⓒ the English
   - Ⓓ Thomas Telford

3. What was macadam?
   - Ⓐ a type of sand used in road building
   - Ⓑ a stone used by the Incas
   - Ⓒ a mixture of stone and tar
   - Ⓓ a road in Scotland

4. What were Roman roads like? Write one or two sentences to describe them.

   _____
   _____

5. Who built modern roads in England?

   _____

Name _____ Date _____

Directions: *Read the passage. Then use the information from the passage to answer questions 1–5.*

# Exploring the Deep

At 29,030 feet, Mount Everest is the highest point on Earth. It is in Asia. The highest point in North America is Mount McKinley in Alaska (20,320 feet). Do you know where the lowest point is? If you think about it, you'll realize it has to be in the ocean.

**Challenger Deep**

The lowest point on Earth is called Challenger Deep. It is 36,000 feet below sea level in the Mariana Trench. This is a valley in the Pacific Ocean near the Philippines. In 1960, two men went nearly to the bottom of Challenger Deep in a U.S. Navy submersible. (A submersible is a small underwater craft used for deep ocean exploring.) No one has gone back there since.

**Exploring the Ocean Floor**

Scientists can explore most of the ocean floor in submersibles. But going much deeper than 20,000 feet is very difficult for people. That's what ROVs are used for: to go where people can't. (ROVs are robots used to explore the ocean. They are run remotely from a ship. They take pictures and pick things up.) ROVs like sea-tractors can do things that people can't. (A sea-tractor is an ROV that rolls along the ocean floor.) Some can stay underwater for six months.

**Galápagos Rift**

Another deep place is the Galápagos Rift near Ecuador, in the Pacific Ocean. The rift is 7,500 feet below sea level. In 1977, scientists found something new there—hot springs. They rise from the ocean floor. The water is hot because of nearby volcanoes. All around the springs live strange giant worms. We are still learning how these worms can live without sunlight.

Name _____  Date _____

1. How far below sea level is the bottom of Challenger Deep?
   Ⓐ 7,500 feet
   Ⓑ 20,000 feet
   Ⓒ 29,000 feet
   Ⓓ 36,000 feet

2. What is a <u>sea-tractor</u> used for?
   Ⓐ exploring the ocean floor
   Ⓑ taking pictures of fish
   Ⓒ looking for sunlight
   Ⓓ working on fish farms

3. What is a <u>submersible</u>?
   Ⓐ a strange giant worm
   Ⓑ an underwater hot spring
   Ⓒ an underwater craft used in deep water
   Ⓓ a low point in the ocean

4. What is the Galápagos Rift and where is it located?
   _____
   _____

5. What are ROVs and what can they do?
   _____
   _____

# Comets and Meteors

A comet is a chunk of ice and rock that travels around, or orbits, the sun. Most comets have tails made of dust and gas. Comets may appear bright as they travel through space. The long tail of a bright comet looks like <u>streaming</u> hair. In fact, the word comet comes from a Greek word for "long hair."

Some bright comets pass by Earth on a regular schedule. The most famous of these comets is named for Edmund Halley. He was an English astronomer. Halley studied a comet that he <u>observed</u> in England in 1682.

He believed this comet followed the same path as comets that were seen in 1531 and 1607. He predicted that this same comet would <u>reappear</u> every 76 years. So far, his predictions have come true. Halley's comet last crossed the night sky in 1986.

Meteors are similar to comets. But they do not orbit any object in the solar system. Some people call meteors "shooting stars." Others call them "<u>fireballs</u>." The word *meteor* comes from a Greek word that means "things in the air."

Meteors are really rocks, and some of them do fall to Earth. When they land, they are called meteorites. They look much like other rocks you might find. The Arctic and the Antarctic are places covered with ice and snow. They would be good <u>locations</u> to look for meteorites.

Name _____ Date _____

1. The passage says, "The long tail of a bright comet looks like streaming hair." The word streaming means _____.
   - Ⓐ burning
   - Ⓑ crying
   - Ⓒ flowing
   - Ⓓ cutting

2. Halley observed a comet in England in 1682. What does observed mean?
   - Ⓐ caught
   - Ⓑ named
   - Ⓒ lost
   - Ⓓ saw

3. Halley believed that one comet would reappear every 76 years. The word reappear means _____.
   - Ⓐ be shaped like a pear
   - Ⓑ come back again
   - Ⓒ crash into Earth
   - Ⓓ be equal to something else

4. You can tell that a fireball most likely is _____.
   - Ⓐ round and yellow
   - Ⓑ long and thin
   - Ⓒ cold and green
   - Ⓓ large and soft

5. The passage says that the Arctic and Antarctic would be "good locations to look for meteorites." The word location means _____.
   - Ⓐ weather
   - Ⓑ place
   - Ⓒ time
   - Ⓓ country

# Bird Food

Have you ever heard the <u>expression</u> "free as a bird"? This suggests that a bird's time is its own, but that's not true. Birds spend most of their time working toward one goal: looking for food. Not all birds look for the same kind of food. Some birds, such as owls and eagles, are carnivores. They eat meat. Others are mostly plant eaters, or herbivores. These include the hummingbird and Canada goose. Some birds will eat both meat and plants. These kinds of birds are known as omnivores. Starlings, for example, are <u>omnivorous</u> birds.

How do birds find the food they are always looking for? They mostly use their sharp eyesight. A bird's eyes are important for its survival. The bird that boasts the biggest eyeballs is the ostrich. Its eyes are two inches across. But the owl is the bird with the best night vision. Owls can also claim another <u>notable</u> trait: they have the best hearing. <u>Exceptional</u> night vision and acute hearing allow owls to hunt for food at night.

The different eating habits of birds can affect other aspects of nature. For example, insect-eating birds help control the insect population. Others, such as the hummingbird, spread pollen and help flowering plants <u>reproduce</u>.

Name _____ Date_____

1. The passage says, "Have you ever heard the expression 'free as a bird'?" What is an **expression**?
   - Ⓐ a joke or riddle
   - Ⓑ the ability to express
   - Ⓒ a saying
   - Ⓓ something full of expression

2. Starlings are **omnivorous** birds. What does **omnivorous** mean?
   - Ⓐ free
   - Ⓑ hardworking
   - Ⓒ active at night
   - Ⓓ both plant- and meat-eating

3. "Owls can also claim another **notable** trait." The word **notable** means _____.
   - Ⓐ worth noting
   - Ⓑ in a note
   - Ⓒ note again
   - Ⓓ without a note

4. Owls have **exceptional** night vision. The word **exceptional** means _____.
   - Ⓐ normal
   - Ⓑ not very good
   - Ⓒ below normal
   - Ⓓ unusually good

5. Hummingbirds help flowering plants **reproduce**. The word **reproduce** means _____.
   - Ⓐ lose flowers
   - Ⓑ make more plants
   - Ⓒ become colorful
   - Ⓓ move to new places

# Magic Math Figures

Long ago, people thought that numbers could have magical powers. For example, some people believed that the numbers in a magic square could <u>thwart</u> disease and keep people healthy. Although that was not true, through the ages people have <u>amused</u> themselves with magic squares and other entertaining math figures, such as magic triangles and magic daisies.

## Magic Squares

Look at the magic square shown on the right. Add the numbers in each row going across, up and down, and <u>diagonally</u>. Do you come up with the same answer of 15 for each row? That's amazing!

## Magic Triangles

Here is a <u>challenge</u> for you. It will not be easy. First, draw a triangle like the one shown here. In each circle along the sides of the triangle, write a number from 4 through 9. Here's where the magic comes in. Write the numbers along each side of the triangle so they add up to 21.

## Magic Daisies

Was your magic triangle a success? If so, you might want to <u>attempt</u> to figure out the numbers that make up a magic daisy. At the center of the daisy, write the number 6. Then write one number from 1 through 11 in each circle. The numbers in each line should add up to 18.

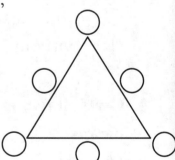

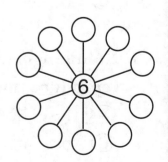

Name _____ Date_____

1. The passage says, "Some people believed that the numbers in a magic square could <u>thwart</u> disease." What does the word <u>thwart</u> mean?
   - Ⓐ cause to spread
   - Ⓑ find a cure for
   - Ⓒ prevent from happening
   - Ⓓ think about

2. Through the ages people have <u>amused</u> themselves with magic squares. The word <u>amused</u> means _____.
   - Ⓐ bothered
   - Ⓑ had fun
   - Ⓒ prepared
   - Ⓓ caused trouble

3. In the magic square, you add the numbers <u>diagonally</u>. What clues in the passage help you know that <u>diagonally</u> means "at a slant"?
   _____
   _____

4. "Here is a <u>challenge</u> for you." What clues in the passage help you know that a <u>challenge</u> is "a difficult task"?
   _____
   _____

5. The word <u>attempt</u> means _____.
   - Ⓐ draw
   - Ⓑ explore
   - Ⓒ try
   - Ⓓ quit

©2015 Benchmark Education Company, LLC

# Surviving Winter

When winter comes, people tend to stay indoors and turn on the heat. But how do wild animals survive winter?

Animals adapt to cold in various ways. Squirrels, for example, eat more food in the fall to gain an extra layer of fat. When food is hard to find in winter, their bodies burn this fat to keep warm. Squirrels also grow thick fur coats. They find holes in trees or in the ground and then huddle together to stay warm. Five squirrels close together stay warmer than one squirrel all by itself.

Chipmunks are different from most squirrels. When it gets very cold, chipmunks hibernate. As they go into a special deep sleep, their heart rate and breathing slow down. Their body temperature goes from 98 to 43 degrees Fahrenheit. Hibernating helps them save body heat. When it warms up a bit, chipmunks wake up again.

Birds adapt to cold, too. They can fluff up their feathers to trap additional layers of warm air next to their bodies. They face into the wind so cold air can't get under their feathers. But their legs and feet don't have feathers. Some birds stand on one foot. The other foot snuggles up in the feathers to stay warm. Ducks sometimes hunker down right on the ground to keep their feet under them, wrapped in warm feathers.

These are just some of the ways animals survive the winter. The next time it gets cold and you're warm inside, think about how the animals are doing outdoors.

Name _____ Date _____

1. The passage asks, "But how do wild animals <u>survive</u> winter?" What does the word <u>survive</u> mean?
   - Ⓐ play with
   - Ⓑ enjoy
   - Ⓒ live through
   - Ⓓ gather together

2. The passage says, "Animals adapt to cold in <u>various</u> ways." What does the word <u>various</u> mean?
   - Ⓐ different
   - Ⓑ clever
   - Ⓒ unusual
   - Ⓓ silly

3. "When it gets very cold, chipmunks <u>hibernate</u>." What clues in the passage help you understand the meaning of <u>hibernate</u>?
   _____
   _____

4. Birds fluff up their feathers to trap <u>additional</u> layers of warm air. What does <u>additional</u> mean?
   - Ⓐ small
   - Ⓑ costly
   - Ⓒ heavy
   - Ⓓ extra

5. Ducks sometimes <u>hunker</u>. What clues in the passage help you understand the meaning of <u>hunker</u>?
   _____
   _____

©2015 Benchmark Education Company, LLC

Name _____ Date _____

Directions: Read the passage. Then use the information from the passage to answer questions 1–5.

# Underground Buildings

Buildings are always built aboveground, right? Wrong. Over 300 public buildings in the United States are underground. More than 5,000 families live in underground homes. Some are <u>completely</u> under the ground. Others are built into hillsides and are not totally buried.

One of these is the Capitol Visitor Center in Washington, D.C. Thousands of people visit the Capitol each day. The visitor <u>center</u> certainly has room for all of them. There are theaters and gift shops in the building.

Another underground complex is Zankel Hall in New York. This concert hall seats 644 people. Other kinds of underground buildings are museums, libraries, and malls.

Many people like underground houses because they are <u>easy</u> to take care of. On hot days, they are cool. They are easy to heat. They are quieter, too. There is little or no outside noise in an underground house.

There are several reasons why some people build downward instead of skyward. One is that an underground building does not get in the way of open spaces. A playground or a park could be right above the building.

There will be more underground buildings in the future. But they won't take the place of <u>ordinary</u> buildings. People may need to get used to the idea of working and living underground. It can be difficult for some people to live comfortably without natural light.

Name _____ Date _____

1. The passage says, "Some are <u>completely</u> under the ground."
   Which word from the passage means about the same as <u>completely</u>?
   - Ⓐ always
   - Ⓑ certainly
   - Ⓒ totally
   - Ⓓ comfortably

2. They are <u>easy</u> to take care of. Which word from the passage means the opposite of <u>easy</u>?
   - Ⓐ natural
   - Ⓑ difficult
   - Ⓒ other
   - Ⓓ quieter

3. They won't take the place of <u>ordinary</u> buildings. Which word is an antonym for <u>ordinary</u>?
   - Ⓐ unusual
   - Ⓑ common
   - Ⓒ daily
   - Ⓓ little

4. "The visitor <u>center</u> certainly has room for all of them."
   Which word from the passage means about the same as <u>center</u>?
   - Ⓐ noise
   - Ⓑ hillside
   - Ⓒ concert
   - Ⓓ complex

5. In which sentence is the underlined word used correctly?
   - Ⓐ How much does each building stone <u>way</u>?
   - Ⓑ Being underground can <u>way</u> on your mind.
   - Ⓒ That is the best <u>way</u> to heat a home.
   - Ⓓ His newest building is the color of <u>way</u>.

Name _____ Date _____

Directions: Read the passage. Then use the information from the passage to answer questions 1–5.

# The Power of Magma

Deep inside Earth, it is so hot that rock can melt. When rock melts, it turns into magma. Magma is lighter than the cooler rock around it, so it rises and <u>collects</u> in pools. Sometimes pools of melted rock push through cracks in the earth. This is how a volcano erupts.

Some magma is thin and comes out of the earth slowly. People and other animals can escape from it. But sometimes magma is <u>dense</u> and sticky. Air gets trapped below it. Then pressure builds until suddenly very hot magma and air blow out of the volcano. This kind of eruption is <u>dangerous</u>.

Can something so dangerous be <u>useful</u> to people? The people of Iceland have used heat from magma for years. Iceland is an island in the North Atlantic Ocean. It has volcanoes and lots of magma not far under the ground. Water heated by magma rises in the earth. Then this hot water is piped all over the island. Most of Iceland's houses and other buildings are heated this way.

In other places, water heated by magma is piped under roads and sidewalks. This keeps the roads from getting icy when the weather is freezing. It doesn't cost much to heat roads and houses this way. The low cost could almost make you wish you had a volcano nearby!

Name _____ Date _____

1. The passage says, "It rises and collects in pools." Which word means about the same as collects?
   - Ⓐ swims
   - Ⓑ cools
   - Ⓒ gathers
   - Ⓓ explodes

2. But sometimes magma is dense. Which word from the passage means the opposite of dense?
   - Ⓐ hot
   - Ⓑ below
   - Ⓒ thin
   - Ⓓ freezing

3. Which sentence uses the underlined word correctly?
   - Ⓐ Water was pumped through the pipes.
   - Ⓑ Are you threw with dinner?
   - Ⓒ The volcano through rocks and dust into the air.
   - Ⓓ I read threw the whole book.

4. The passage says, "This kind of eruption is dangerous." Which word means the opposite of dangerous?
   - Ⓐ risky
   - Ⓑ safe
   - Ⓒ warm
   - Ⓓ costly

5. "Can something so dangerous be useful to people?" Which word means about the same as useful?
   - Ⓐ awful
   - Ⓑ careful
   - Ⓒ hopeful
   - Ⓓ helpful

## Ongoing Comprehension Strategy Assessment • 41

Name _____ Date _____

Directions: Read the passage. Then use the information from the passage to answer questions 1–5.

# Windmills

The first windmills appeared in Persia, in the Middle East, around A.D 600. Before the wind was used to <u>drive</u> windmills, humans or other animals provided the strength to turn a grinding stone. Farmers placed grain or corn between two stones and ground it into flour.

These first windmills were built on their sides. The whole thing turned in the wind. A sail or <u>blade</u> at one end caught the force of the wind and made the stone spin. Later designs turned the windmill on end so that it was higher and could catch more wind. On the upright windmill, only the blades or sails turned in the wind. Different parts transferred this motion to a grinding stone.

Windmills soon spread to Europe. People in Holland saw more than one use for this power. They used it to grind corn, but they also used it to pump water. The Dutch used windmills to <u>drain</u> their low fields. Then they built dams and dikes to keep the water away from farmland.

Better designs have improved these simple windmills. Today, windmills can spin faster. They can <u>stand</u> the beating they take from the wind. Some look like giant airplane propellers. They spin even in a slight breeze.

Windmills that create electrical power are called wind turbines. Over 16,000 wind turbines have been placed where a strong and steady source of wind blows. They can produce enough electricity to power a city the size of San Francisco for a year. The U.S. government estimates that windmills could <u>fill</u> one-fifth of the nation's demand for electricity.

Name _____ Date _____

1. The wind was used to <u>drive</u> windmills. What does <u>drive</u> mean in this sentence?
   - Ⓐ steer a car
   - Ⓑ hit with force
   - Ⓒ cause to move
   - Ⓓ a road for cars

2. "A sail or <u>blade</u> at one end caught the force of the wind." In which sentence is the word <u>blade</u> used in the same way?
   - Ⓐ The <u>blade</u> on his skate is dull.
   - Ⓑ Mr. Collins cut his finger on the <u>blade</u> of a knife.
   - Ⓒ She put a <u>blade</u> of grass between her thumbs.
   - Ⓓ One <u>blade</u> on the ceiling fan broke yesterday.

3. "The Dutch used windmills to <u>drain</u> their low fields." What does <u>drain</u> mean as it is used in this sentence?
   - Ⓐ a pipe for water
   - Ⓑ draw water from
   - Ⓒ a loss of resources
   - Ⓓ take energy from

4. "They can <u>stand</u> the beating they take from the wind." What does <u>stand</u> mean in this sentence?
   - Ⓐ put up with
   - Ⓑ rise to one's feet
   - Ⓒ rest in one place
   - Ⓓ a raised platform

5. "Windmills could <u>fill</u> one-fifth of the nation's demand for electricity." Which sentence uses the word <u>fill</u> in the same way?
   - Ⓐ That new store will <u>fill</u> the need for groceries.
   - Ⓑ Mrs. Brownell needs five tons of <u>fill</u> for her yard.
   - Ⓒ Most of the <u>fill</u> came out of the pillows.
   - Ⓓ I have had my <u>fill</u> of his silly excuses.

Name _____ Date _____

Directions: Read the passage. Then use the information from the passage to answer questions 1–5.

# Growing Spuds

What has many eyes but cannot see?
A potato!

Potatoes taste great no matter how you prepare them—fried, boiled, mashed, or baked. Everyone likes spuds, but did you know they're also quite easy to grow? You can take potatoes from your kitchen, put them in the ground, and produce new potato plants!

Potatoes grow underground. They need loose soil to grow, but they do not like rocks or stones. So first, till the soil to remove all the stones. Then dig a trench six inches deep and six inches wide.

Cut some old potatoes into pieces, making sure that each piece has at least one "eye." (The little dimples in a potato are called eyes, and each eye will become a potato plant.) Put the pieces in your trench one foot apart, and pile four inches of dirt into the trench.

Before long, little green shoots will emerge from the earth. Water them if it doesn't rain. When the plants are six inches high, pile more dirt around them. Potatoes are already growing under the ground. If the sun hits the potatoes, their skins will turn green, and green skin is not good to eat. When the plants are one foot tall, put more dirt around them.

Your potato plants will soon become small green bushes. When the bushes produce white flowers, you can start looking for new potatoes. Just dig down a little with your fingers to find them. These tiny potatoes taste good boiled and eaten with butter, and you don't even need to peel them. For big potatoes, you'll have to wait a bit longer. They will be ready when the plants turn brown.

Name _____ Date _____

1. The passage says, "So first, <u>till</u> the soil to remove all the stones." What does the word <u>till</u> mean in this sentence?
   - Ⓐ up to the time of
   - Ⓑ prepare by raking
   - Ⓒ steer with a rudder
   - Ⓓ a drawer for money

2. The passage says, "Each eye will become a potato <u>plant</u>." Which sentence uses the word <u>plant</u> in the same way?
   - Ⓐ We live near the power <u>plant</u>.
   - Ⓑ Tomorrow we will <u>plant</u> apple trees.
   - Ⓒ A new <u>plant</u> is growing next to the path.
   - Ⓓ Spring is the best time to <u>plant</u> vegetables.

3. The passage says, "Before long, little green <u>shoots</u> will emerge from the earth." What does the word <u>shoots</u> mean in this sentence?
   - Ⓐ new or young plants
   - Ⓑ uses a gun
   - Ⓒ sessions of filming for a movie
   - Ⓓ moves suddenly or quickly

4. The plants are one <u>foot</u> tall. What does <u>foot</u> mean in this sentence?
   - Ⓐ part of the leg
   - Ⓑ a unit of measure
   - Ⓒ to pay for
   - Ⓓ the end of a bed

5. The passage says, "For big potatoes, you'll have to wait a <u>bit</u> longer." Which sentence uses the word <u>bit</u> in the same way?
   - Ⓐ Two boys acted out a short <u>bit</u> involving a parrot.
   - Ⓑ Henry <u>bit</u> into the apple.
   - Ⓒ She put the <u>bit</u> into the horse's mouth.
   - Ⓓ I feel a <u>bit</u> better now.

# Midyear Test

**Grasshopper and Toad** .................................................. 124

**Eating Bugs** ............................................................ 126

**Sam's Journal** ......................................................... 128

**A Young Champion** ..................................................... 130

**Science to the Rescue** ................................................. 132

**Learning to Think** ..................................................... 134

**Jackstones** ............................................................ 136

# Midyear Test Answer Key

1. C
2. B
3. A
4. D
5. A
6. B
7. C
8. A
9. D
10. C
11. A
12. D
13. C
14. B
15. D
16. C
17. A
18. D
19. B
20. D
21. B
22. C
23. A
24. D
25. D
26. B
27. D
28. A
29. A
30. C
31. A
32. C
33. D
34. A
35. C
36. C

# Grasshopper and Toad

Long ago, Grasshopper and Toad were good friends. They did a lot of things together, but they had never shared a meal. One day, Toad asked, "Grasshopper, will you come to my house for dinner? We'll have a delicious feast."

When Grasshopper arrived, he and Toad washed their forelegs in the water jar. Grasshopper's legs rubbed together and made a chirping noise, and the noise annoyed Toad. He frowned and said, "Grasshopper, you'll have to stop that chirping. How can I eat if I have to listen to that racket?"

Grasshopper tried to eat quietly but couldn't. His legs always rubbed together, and each time, Toad complained.

Grasshopper was upset and couldn't eat his food. When Toad finished, Grasshopper asked, "Toad, will you come to my house for dinner tomorrow?"

The next day at Grasshopper's house, he and Toad again washed in a water jar, but Grasshopper stopped Toad before he could eat. He said, "Go back and wash again. You are filthy from hopping in the dirt."

Toad cleansed his legs again and hopped back to the table. Toad reached out to pick up a plate, but Grasshopper glared at him and said, "Don't put your dirty hands in the food. You need to wash them again."

Toad became furious. "Why did you invite me to dinner if you don't want to eat with me? You know I hop on my legs, and I can't help it if they get dirty when I hop to the table."

Grasshopper was still angry from the day before. "You started it yesterday! You know I can't eat without chirping."

Toad left in a huff, and from that day forward, Grasshopper and Toad were no longer friends.

Name _____ Date _____

1. In the passage, Toad says, "How can I eat if I have to listen to that <u>racket</u>?" Which word means the same as <u>racket</u>?
   - Ⓐ quiet hum
   - Ⓑ wooden bat
   - Ⓒ loud noise
   - Ⓓ croaking sound

2. Why did Grasshopper and Toad first decide to share a meal?
   - Ⓐ They didn't have enough food to eat alone.
   - Ⓑ They were good friends.
   - Ⓒ They ate the same kinds of food.
   - Ⓓ They wanted to show off their houses.

3. Which words best describe the characters of both Grasshopper and Toad in this story?
   - Ⓐ stubborn and easily bothered
   - Ⓑ relaxed and friendly
   - Ⓒ serious and usually quiet
   - Ⓓ happy and carefree

4. What is the problem in this story?
   - Ⓐ Grasshopper loves to make chirping noises.
   - Ⓑ Toad doesn't like Grasshopper's food.
   - Ⓒ The friends don't want to eat when they are dirty.
   - Ⓓ Grasshopper and Toad don't accept each other as they are.

5. The passage says, "Toad left <u>in a huff</u>." What does <u>in a huff</u> mean?
   - Ⓐ angrily
   - Ⓑ early
   - Ⓒ in fear
   - Ⓓ slowly

# Midyear Test

Name _____ Date _____

Directions: Read the passage. Then use the information from the passage to answer questions 6–10.

## Eating Bugs

How about a nice bowl of ants for breakfast? Maybe some fried crickets for lunch? You can have worm cookies for dessert. Do these sound good?

No, this isn't a nightmare or a horror movie. Some scientists think that growing and eating bugs will be important in the future.

The world's population is growing fast. People need to find new ways to get food. Scientists suggest eating bugs for many reasons. One is that insects need less food than other animals. Cattle and other livestock are warm-blooded animals. When they eat, they use a lot of energy to stay warm. Insects are cold-blooded. They grow quickly without wasting energy on staying warm. For example, silkworms grow two to three times as much as cattle by eating the same amount of feed. Many other insects are the same.

Bugs aren't picky about what they eat, either. They can grow by eating cardboard, animal waste, and leftovers from food plants. Eating bugs is good for you, too. Most insects provide more protein per pound than chicken. They are also rich in minerals such as iron.

Today, insects are grown for food in Thailand and other parts of Asia. They are used in Africa, too. But few Americans want to try eating bugs. People think bugs are dirty and might be poisonous. They imagine eating the whole bug, including the head, scratchy legs, and body. That doesn't sound like a good meal. But we don't have to eat the whole bug. We can eat just the "meaty" part, and that can be prepared in many ways. One choice is to create a "bug nugget." It doesn't look like a bug any more than a chicken nugget looks like a chicken. Besides, it might even taste good.

So if someone tells you to go eat bugs, give them a try. Just be sure they're prepared the right way!

Name _____ Date _____

6. What is the main idea of the third paragraph in this passage?
   - Ⓐ Bugs can taste good if they are prepared the right way.
   - Ⓑ Insects grow quickly and need less food than other animals.
   - Ⓒ Scientists want to force bugs to grow more quickly.
   - Ⓓ Only certain kinds of insects are good for eating.

7. The passage says, "Most insects provide more protein per <u>pound</u> than chicken." Which of these sentences uses the word <u>pound</u> in the same way?
   - Ⓐ Use a hammer to pound in that nail.
   - Ⓑ Trevor likes to pound on the drum.
   - Ⓒ This little puppy weighs less than a pound.
   - Ⓓ We got our new pet from the pound.

8. What would be another good title for this passage?
   - Ⓐ "A New Source of Food"
   - Ⓑ "American Bugs"
   - Ⓒ "Cattle and Other Livestock"
   - Ⓓ "The Whole Bug"

9. From the author's view, what is probably the worst thing about the idea of using bugs as food?
   - Ⓐ having cookies for dessert
   - Ⓑ making bug nuggets
   - Ⓒ getting lots of protein
   - Ⓓ eating the heads and legs

10. The passage says, "People think bugs are dirty and might be <u>poisonous</u>." What does <u>poisonous</u> mean?
    - Ⓐ tasty
    - Ⓑ healthy
    - Ⓒ harmful
    - Ⓓ colorful

# Sam's Journal

**June 23**

My parents told me a while ago that we would be going to Yellowstone National Park, and we are finally on our way. I've been as high as a kite all week! The flight to Jackson, Wyoming, was fun. They gave us lots of snacks.

**June 24**

It's hard to describe the smell here. People say it smells like rotten eggs. I've never smelled a rotten egg, but the smell is bad. My little sister, Francine, keeps making gagging noises and pretends she's going to throw up on me. She's pretty funny. A ranger explained that the smell comes from the sulfur in the hot springs. We watched the Old Faithful geyser today. While we were there, it erupted twice in 72 minutes. It doesn't really erupt every hour, but it's pretty close.

**June 25**

We left to see Giant Geyser today. It sends a spray more than 250 feet in the air. On the way, we had to stop our car for a herd of buffalo in the road. Francine was about to open the door and get out. She thought they looked furry and friendly, but I grabbed her. The ranger said that buffalo can be dangerous. They can run a lot faster than people—up to 30 miles an hour! There aren't any fences in the park, and we've seen big herds of elk. Today, a bald eagle circled over our heads. The rangers say that this is where the animals live and the people are just visitors.

**June 26**

I learned why there are so many hot springs and geysers here. In most places, Earth's crust is about 20 miles thick. But in Yellowstone, it's only about two miles thick. The ground is closer to Earth's core, which is very hot. In some places, the ground is so hot you can't touch it. Today is our last day here. I wish we could stay longer.

Name _____ Date_____

**11.** What will most likely happen tomorrow?
- Ⓐ Sam and his family will go home.
- Ⓑ Sam will go to see Old Faithful again.
- Ⓒ Sam and his sister will go hiking.
- Ⓓ Sam will walk near the buffalo.

**12.** Why did Francine keep pretending to throw up?
- Ⓐ She did not feel well.
- Ⓑ She wanted to go home.
- Ⓒ She was too close to the animals.
- Ⓓ She wanted to make Sam laugh.

**13.** Why did Sam grab Francine when she started to open the car door near the buffalo?
- Ⓐ He wanted his parents to keep driving.
- Ⓑ He wanted her to see the eagle instead.
- Ⓒ He didn't want her to get hurt.
- Ⓓ He didn't want her to scare the buffalo.

**14.** How was June 23 different from the other days?
- Ⓐ The family saw geysers that day.
- Ⓑ They flew on a plane that day.
- Ⓒ The family went sightseeing that day.
- Ⓓ Sam did not write in his journal that day.

**15.** From the passage, you can infer that Sam _____.
- Ⓐ was bothered by Francine
- Ⓑ was bored on vacation
- Ⓒ feared wild animals
- Ⓓ listened closely to the rangers

## Midyear Test

Name _____ Date _____

Directions: Read the passage. Then use the information from the passage to answer questions 16–20.

# A Young Champion

It was the 2013 Australian Open. Nineteen-year-old Sloane Stephens tossed the ball high. She was up against the legend Serena Williams, one of her heroes. If she won, it would be her biggest victory yet. All eyes were on Stephens as her tennis racket made contact and sent the ball flying over the net.

Sloane Stephens was born on March 20, 1993, in Florida. Her parents divorced when she was young. At nine, Stephens played tennis for the first time. Her days were spent at Saviano High Performance Tennis Academy, where she honed her skills outside of school. At age 16, she turned professional, but suffered the loss of her father.

While she waited to turn 18, Stephens competed in the Junior League Grand Slam against the top athletes her age. Her determination paid off! She won three out of four of her Junior Grand Slam Doubles matches.

The next year, in 2011, Sloane Stephens made it to the U.S. Open. There she advanced all the way to the semifinals before being defeated by Ana Ivanovic. The Women's Tennis Association recognized her as one of the top 100 tennis players in the world. In 2012, Stephens went on to become the youngest player to have competed in all four Grand Slams!

By the time of the 2013 Australian Open, Stephens was considered the future of American tennis. The morning of her match against Serena Williams, she told herself, "Go out and play and do your best." She did just that, battling Williams with powerful swings from the baseline. Underdog Sloane Stephens played with skill and poise.

When Serena Williams's return did not make it across the net, Stephens's eyes grew wide. A smile crept across her face. The tennis court echoed with cheers from the audience. She had won! At the net, Williams shook Stephens's hand as they both agreed it was a "good game."

Name _____ Date _____

16. The passage says, "Her days were spent at Saviano High Performance Tennis Academy, where she honed her skills outside of school." The word honed means _____.
    Ⓐ  knew
    Ⓑ  balanced
    Ⓒ  perfected
    Ⓓ  paid

17. In this passage, the purpose of the fifth paragraph is to _____.
    Ⓐ  describe the way Sloane Stephens will solve a problem
    Ⓑ  compare and contrast female and male tennis players
    Ⓒ  explain the purpose of the 2013 Australian Open
    Ⓓ  give the author's opinion of Serena Williams

18. What evidence supports the statement that in 2013 Sloan Stephens "was considered the future of American tennis"?
    Ⓐ  She started playing tennis as early as age nine.
    Ⓑ  She continued to play tennis after she lost her father.
    Ⓒ  She was age nineteen when the Australian Open started.
    Ⓓ  She had already played in four Grand Slam tournaments.

19. From this passage, what can you conclude about the tennis career of Sloane Stephens?
    Ⓐ  She will win more tennis matches than will Serena Williams.
    Ⓑ  Hard work and determination helped Stephens win at tennis..
    Ⓒ  The Australian Open may be the only tournament Stephens can win again.
    Ⓓ  If Stephens had been older, she would have beaten Ana Ivanovic.

20. The passage says, "A smile crept across her face." What does crept across her face mean?
    Ⓐ  Stephens did most things slowly but carefully.
    Ⓑ  Stephens smiled only when people asked her to.
    Ⓒ  Stephens smiled as she crept off the tennis court.
    Ⓓ  Stephens smiled when she realized her success.

# Science to the Rescue

On August 5, 2010, an explosion trapped 33 miners 2,300 feet underground in Chile. Sixty-nine days later, the miners were pulled to the top. Some people called the rescue a miracle. Much of it depended on science and technology.

**Drilling**

Rescuers drilled down thousands of feet to reach the miners. But scientists helped them hit the target. The drill needed to be in just the right position. If it were tipped just a tiny bit, it would miss the target badly. First, two small holes were drilled to provide air, food, water, and clothing to the miners. The holes were lined with steel. Long, thin pods, less than 5 inches (12.5 centimeters) wide, carried supplies up and down.

**The Mine Rescue**

The miners needed a larger hole to be rescued. A small hole was drilled first, and then a larger drill slowly made it wider. The drill worked day and night. It drilled down about 20 feet (6 meters) each day. It made the hole 26 inches (65 centimeters) wide. As it drilled down, rocks and dirt fell down the hole. The miners worked around the clock, too. They moved about 1,000 pounds (454 kilograms) of rock away from the hole each hour.

**The Rescue Capsule**

Scientists from the space program in the United States gave advice on building the rescue capsule. It contained oxygen tanks for breathing. It also included a safety harness and communication device.

When the miners finally came up, their eyes had to be protected from the bright sun. But they were generally healthy. With the help of science, all of the

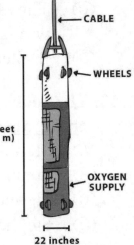

RESCUE CAPSULE
— CABLE
— WHEELS
15 feet (4.5 m)
OXYGEN SUPPLY
22 inches (55 cm)

Name _____ Date_____

21. Which is the best summary of this passage?
   Ⓐ Finding the miners alive in Chile was a miracle.
   Ⓑ Rescuing the miners depended on science and technology.
   Ⓒ Working in underground mines is a dangerous job.
   Ⓓ The United States provided a lot of help in the rescue.

22. In which part of the passage can you find how wide the supply pods were?
   Ⓐ the first paragraph
   Ⓑ **The Mine Rescue**
   Ⓒ **Drilling**
   Ⓓ **The Rescue Capsule**

23. Where is the oxygen supply located in the rescue capsule?
   Ⓐ at the bottom
   Ⓑ at the top
   Ⓒ on the miner's back
   Ⓓ between the miner's feet

24. How deep were the miners trapped?
   Ⓐ 69 feet deep
   Ⓑ a few hundred feet deep
   Ⓒ 1,000 feet deep
   Ⓓ 2,300 feet deep

25. The author's purpose in this passage is to _____.
   Ⓐ describe how brave the miners were
   Ⓑ explain the importance of mining
   Ⓒ discuss the laws covering mine safety
   Ⓓ give information about a mine rescue

Directions: Read the passage. Then use the information from the passage to answer questions 26–30.

# Learning to Think by Horace Sanders

I'll never forget how Mr. Grant looked when I first studied him. It seemed like his eyes were smiling a little. He looked like he knew some things I did not, but he'd be glad to share them.

Almost everyone in our class in elementary school went to the after-school program. The recreation center was in even worse shape than our school. It had two floors and an outdoor basketball court with rusty backboards. But we spent hours there, playing every game you could think of. Mr. Grant would usually shoot a few baskets. But before long he'd be back inside in his own room. It had a couple of folding tables covered in chessboards. The blackboard had a permanent picture of a chessboard on it.

He would play a game of chess and explain all the moves. He taught us how the pieces moved, what "check" meant, and some ways to start the game. Before I knew it, I was hooked. Sometimes, I'd go right to the chess room because I'd been thinking about a chess problem all day.

Mr. Grant <u>established</u> a chess club for boys and girls of all ages. We played against teams from other parts of the city. In high school, we even played in a state championship. Mr. Grant was always teaching us, even when we got good enough to beat him sometimes.

Today, I run my own company with more than 100 employees. I think a lot of my success began with Mr. Grant and chess. He taught me to think ahead and plan my actions. In chess, I had to consider several options and decide on the best one, just as I do in business. Mr. Grant wasn't really just teaching us how to play chess. He was teaching us how to think. I'll always be grateful for how he took some rough young kids and turned them into thinkers.

Name _____  Date _____

**26.** What can you tell about the neighborhood where the author grew up?
- Ⓐ It was in a rural area.
- Ⓑ It was poor and rundown.
- Ⓒ It had excellent schools.
- Ⓓ It had a lot of parks and playgrounds.

**27.** The author thinks learning to play chess helped him to _____.
- Ⓐ understand how other people think
- Ⓑ find the right college
- Ⓒ get along better with his friends
- Ⓓ run a successful business

**28.** The passage says, "Mr. Grant <u>established</u> a chess club for boys and girls of all ages." The word <u>established</u> means _____.
- Ⓐ set up
- Ⓑ advertised
- Ⓒ announced
- Ⓓ supported

**29.** Which sentence best describes the character of Mr. Grant?
- Ⓐ He wanted to help his students learn and grow.
- Ⓑ He didn't care about basketball or other sports.
- Ⓒ He almost always had a big smile on his face.
- Ⓓ He only wanted the smartest kids to play chess.

**30.** The author probably wrote this passage because he _____.
- Ⓐ thinks that everyone should learn to play chess
- Ⓑ hopes that people will build a new recreation center
- Ⓒ wants people to know what Mr. Grant did
- Ⓓ feels proud of his own business and his success

# Midyear Test

Name _____ Date _____

Directions: Read the passage. Then use the information from the passage to answer questions 31–36.

# Jackstones

During colonial times, children played a game called "jackstones." They enjoyed it so much they would play until the cows came home. Today, the game is called "jacks." It is played with a rubber ball. It's a snap to pick up and lots of fun.

In the old days, children used one larger, rounded stone and five or six smaller ones. The smaller stones were called jackstones. Sometimes children used other things, such as seeds or sticks.

**How to Play:**

1. One player throws the jackstones on the floor or the ground. The player then throws the larger stone in the air. He or she picks up one jackstone and then catches the larger stone in the same <u>hand</u> before it hits the ground. The player continues with the other stones one at a time in the same way.
2. If each single stone is picked up successfully, the player moves on to pick up two at a time. Each time a player <u>succeeds</u>, he or she moves up to the next number—"threes," "fours," and so on. The winner is the player who advances to pick up all the stones in one try.

jackstones  modern jacks

3. Sometimes there aren't enough stones left for threes or fours. Then the player picks up the remaining stones in one try. For example, a player might pick up three on the first try. Then there are only two left. The last two are picked up in one try.
4. A player fails when the large stone hits the ground or the player picks up the wrong number of jackstones. That player's turn ends. The next player begins with "ones."

Name _____ Date _____

31. The passage says, "They enjoyed it so much they would play until the cows came home." This sentence means that they played _____.
    - Ⓐ for hours and hours
    - Ⓑ in the barn near the cows
    - Ⓒ before they did their chores
    - Ⓓ only on farms

32. The passage says that the player "catches the larger stone in the same <u>hand</u>." Which sentence uses the word <u>hand</u> in the same way?
    - Ⓐ Please deal another hand of cards.
    - Ⓑ Could you hand me that pen?
    - Ⓒ Mia held the key in her hand.
    - Ⓓ On Friday, I gave Dad a hand.

33. The passage says, "It's a snap to pick up and lots of fun." This sentence means that _____.
    - Ⓐ sometimes the pieces break
    - Ⓑ people snap their fingers
    - Ⓒ the stones make a snapping noise
    - Ⓓ the game is easy to learn

34. Before beginning "fours," a player must _____.
    - Ⓐ pick up the jacks three at a time successfully
    - Ⓑ wait until another player has completed "threes"
    - Ⓒ toss the larger stone in the air and catch it three times in a row
    - Ⓓ stop the other players from completing "threes"

35. The passage says, "Each time a player <u>succeeds</u>, he or she moves up to the next number." Which word in the passage means the opposite of <u>succeeds</u>?
    - Ⓐ picks
    - Ⓑ throws
    - Ⓒ fails
    - Ⓓ advances

36. What happens when a player makes a mistake?
    - Ⓐ The player loses the game.
    - Ⓑ The player must begin again at "ones."
    - Ⓒ The player's turn is over.
    - Ⓓ The player must pick up all the jacks.

## Posttest

**Why the Bear Has No Tail** .................................................. 140

**Castles** ............................................................................. 142

**My Trip to India** ............................................................... 144

**Daniel Pinkwater: Writer and Kid** ..................................... 146

**Glaciers** ........................................................................... 148

**Campaign Speech: July 15** ............................................... 150

**An Interview with Aunt Etta** ............................................. 152

# Posttest Answer Key

1. C
2. A
3. D
4. B
5. C
6. D
7. A
8. A
9. D
10. B
11. C
12. D
13. A
14. B
15. C
16. D
17. B
18. A
19. B
20. D
21. B
22. C
23. C
24. D
25. A
26. A
27. C
28. B
29. B
30. D
31. C
32. B
33. A
34. D
35. B
36. C

**Posttest**

Name _____ Date _____

Directions: Read the passage. Then use the information from the passage to answer questions 1–5.

# Why the Bear Has No Tail

One early winter day as Bear wandered through the forest feeling powerfully hungry, he met Fox, who was carrying a large fish.

"Where did you get that wonderful fish?" Bear inquired.

"In the lake," Fox replied, "but you can't have it."

"Oh, I don't want your fish," said Bear, who was now ravenous. Bear hadn't eaten for days, and he was getting impatient. "Just tell me how I can get one for myself."

Now Fox wasn't too keen on Bear catching all the fish in the lake, so he tried to think of a clever ruse. As a very cold wind began to blow from the north, Fox happened on a solution.

"Well, it's pretty easy, once you get the hang of it!" Fox said, chuckling to himself. "Squat down at the edge of the lake backward so your tail dips into the water, and the fish will want to bite it. When you feel the bite, yank your tail out and you'll have a fish!"

Bear peered at Fox's tail to see if this was some kind of trick, but it seemed no worse for wear. So he figured Fox's plan was legitimate.

Bear did just as Fox instructed, but nothing happened for hours. Eventually the lake began to freeze, and Bear's tail became stuck fast in the ice. Bear thought he felt a bite at last, so he pulled and pulled and pulled. Finally, his tail snapped out, but only part of it. All that remained was a tiny stump.

To this very day, bears have only little stumps for tails—and they don't like foxes very much.

Name _____ Date _____

1. The story says, "He tried to think of a clever ruse."
   Which word from the story means about the same as ruse?
   - Ⓐ animal
   - Ⓑ solution
   - Ⓒ trick
   - Ⓓ question

2. Why did Fox trick Bear?
   - Ⓐ He did not want Bear to catch all the fish in the lake.
   - Ⓑ Fox was jealous of Bear's smart plan.
   - Ⓒ He did not want to share his fish with Bear.
   - Ⓓ Fox wanted to keep Bear out of the way for a few hours.

3. Which words best describe the character of Fox in this story?
   - Ⓐ brave and determined
   - Ⓑ honest and hardworking
   - Ⓒ lazy and amusing
   - Ⓓ sneaky and clever

4. What is Bear's problem in this story?
   - Ⓐ He does not like Fox.
   - Ⓑ He has not eaten in days.
   - Ⓒ He has a long tail.
   - Ⓓ He cannot find the lake.

5. The story says that Bear felt ravenous. What does ravenous mean?
   - Ⓐ birdlike
   - Ⓑ bored
   - Ⓒ starving
   - Ⓓ jealous

# Castles

Castles are wonderful tourist attractions nowadays. But there aren't many of them left. Long ago, castles were scattered all over Europe. There were castles in India and some in Japan. The Middle East had castles as well.

People began building castles about 1,000 years ago. In those days, people did not keep their money in banks. Countries did not have police. No one felt <u>safe</u>. People had to protect themselves. So they built castles.

Most castles were made of stone with very high walls. Some castles were built on mountainsides. Others were placed next to water. The water and the mountain helped protect the castle from attack. Moats, or ditches, were dug around the castles and filled with water. Some castles in India were even said to have crocodiles in their moats to keep people away!

Building a castle was <u>expensive</u>. Only wealthy lords and kings could afford them. However, other people depended on the castles. The lord owned the land around the castle, and peasants rented this land. They used it to plant crops. Peasants came inside the castle if there was an attack. They brought all their goods with them, and their cattle, too.

About 500 years ago, many people moved to towns and cities. Countries formed armies for their own defense. People didn't need castles anymore. Rich people still built castles, but not to keep themselves safe. Castles became fancy homes.

Name _____ Date _____

6. According to the passage, which of these places had castles long ago?
   Ⓐ United States
   Ⓑ Canada
   Ⓒ South America
   Ⓓ India

7. The passage says, "No one felt safe." In which of these sentences does the word safe have the same meaning?
   Ⓐ During a storm, you will be safe in the basement.
   Ⓑ Mr. Chase put all the money in the safe.
   Ⓒ The umpire called the base runner safe at home.
   Ⓓ I think that 4,000 is a safe guess.

8. What would be another good title for this passage?
   Ⓐ "Castles Long Ago"
   Ⓑ "How Castles Are Built"
   Ⓒ "Castles of India and Japan"
   Ⓓ "Before the World Changed"

9. From a peasant's view, what was probably the best thing about living near a castle long ago?
   Ⓐ The peasant could rent land for farming.
   Ⓑ The castle was a tourist attraction.
   Ⓒ The peasant could see how the lords lived.
   Ⓓ The castle offered protection from attack.

10. The passage says, "Building a castle was expensive." What does expensive mean?
    Ⓐ dangerous
    Ⓑ costly
    Ⓒ difficult
    Ⓓ cheap

# My Trip to India

**December 20**

The plane ride lasted forever! I, Dorit Maguay, saw three movies before I fell asleep and the flight attendants fed us twice! But finally we made it to Calcutta. I'm so tired, and I want to be in my bed at home. Why did we have to come here? I don't think I like India, and I definitely do not like Indian food. I haven't seen any mac and cheese.

**December 21**

I miss my friends horribly, and I'm here for two more weeks! But today I met my grandmother for the first time. She hugged me until I felt like a pancake, but she had a sad look on her face. I'll ask her why tomorrow.

**December 22**

Grandmother made me some grilled chicken and rice, and it was really good. She said she was sad yesterday because she never gets to see me. I told her, "You're seeing me now!" She laughed at that.

**December 23**

Calcutta is weird. It's different from Los Angeles, anyway! There is much more traffic here, and it's so noisy! Horns honk constantly, and there are so many people! Where do they all come from? It's funny, though—the people are really friendly. I met some of my cousins today.

**December 24**

Mother wears jeans at home, but she wears a sari here. A sari is a dress made from a long piece of cloth. For dinner, my grandmother made dal, a dish made from lentils, which are small brown beans. It tasted okay.

**January 2**

I can't believe we have to go back to Los Angeles. I want to stay here forever! I really like my cousins, and we've had such fun that I don't ever want to leave. Did I mention that I like Indian food now? Macaroni and cheese is okay, but dal is better!

Name _____ Date _____

11. **What will most likely happen next?**
    - Ⓐ Dorit will ask for some mac and cheese.
    - Ⓑ Grandmother will fly home with Dorit.
    - Ⓒ Dorit will return to Los Angeles.
    - Ⓓ Dorit's cousins will convince her to stay in India.

12. **How did Dorit feel toward the end of her visit?**
    - Ⓐ She could not wait to get home.
    - Ⓑ She missed her friends horribly.
    - Ⓒ She could not stand Calcutta anymore.
    - Ⓓ She did not want to leave India.

13. **Dorit probably did not write in her diary from December 24 until January 2 because she was _____.**
    - Ⓐ too busy having fun
    - Ⓑ learning to make Indian food
    - Ⓒ too depressed to write
    - Ⓓ trying to find more paper

14. **How was Calcutta different from Los Angeles?**
    - Ⓐ It was clean and quiet.
    - Ⓑ It was much more crowded.
    - Ⓒ The people were less friendly.
    - Ⓓ There was much less traffic.

15. **The passage says, "She hugged me until I felt like a pancake." What does this sentence mean?**
    - Ⓐ Grandmother had a round, plain face.
    - Ⓑ The pancakes Grandmother made tasted good.
    - Ⓒ Grandmother squeezed her really hard.
    - Ⓓ Grandmother made her want to eat a pancake.

**Posttest**

Name _____ Date _____

Directions: Read the passage. Then use the information from the passage to answer questions 16–20.

# Daniel Pinkwater: Writer and Kid

When Daniel Pinkwater writes for children, he becomes one. He thinks like a child and writes, and he does an <u>extraordinary</u> job.

**When did Daniel Pinkwater begin writing?**

Daniel Pinkwater says he started writing in school. He wrote funny notes to his friends during class, which made them laugh. Of course, Daniel got into trouble.

At school, Daniel learned that writing pays off. He entered a school writing contest and won a free subscription to a magazine.

**What does Daniel write for today?**

Today, Daniel earns money instead of subscriptions by writing books that children love to read. Pinkwater likes his readers, too. He has a Web site called The P-Zone where children can go online and talk to Daniel. They can ask him anything, and he'll reply with an honest answer.

**What is Daniel like at home?**

Daniel Pinkwater works at home with his wife and his dogs. One of his dogs is named Lulu, and he says that Lulu has a dog named Maxine 2. Pinkwater insists that both dogs can read, and he can prove it!

The room where Pinkwater works is quiet. But the room down the hall where his wife illustrates his stories is a zoo. Inside it are barking dogs, meowing cats, and a blaring TV set.

**Is it hard to write books?**

According to Pinkwater, writing a book is very hard work. One picture book took a year to write. On the other hand, a novel can be written more quickly. He says he can write six novels a year. That makes readers happy. They love Daniel Pinkwater's books!

---

**Pinkwater Facts**
**Born:** November 15, 1941
**Home:** Hudson County, New York
**Popular books:**
*The Hoboken Chicken Emergency*
*The Big Orange Splot*
*At the Hotel Larry*
**Where to reach him:**
www.pinkwater.com

Name _____  Date _____

16. The passage says, "He does an extraordinary job." The word extraordinary means _____.

   Ⓐ common
   Ⓑ not very interesting
   Ⓒ very odd
   Ⓓ extremely good

17. Most of the information in this passage is organized by _____.

   Ⓐ time order
   Ⓑ questions and answers
   Ⓒ problems and solutions
   Ⓓ cause and effect

18. Which sentence states an opinion?

   Ⓐ Writing a book is very hard work.
   Ⓑ One picture book took a year to write.
   Ⓒ He can write six novels a year.
   Ⓓ One of his dogs is named Lulu.

19. From the information in this passage, what can you conclude about Daniel Pinkwater and his wife?

   Ⓐ They both love watching TV.
   Ⓑ They both love animals.
   Ⓒ They are both good illustrators.
   Ⓓ They are both good writers.

20. The passage says, "The room down the hall where his wife illustrates his stories is a zoo." What does this sentence mean?

   Ⓐ His wife works at the zoo.
   Ⓑ His wife's room smells like a zoo.
   Ⓒ His wife has many unusual animals.
   Ⓓ His wife's room is very noisy.

# Posttest

Name _____ Date _____

Directions: Read the passage. Then use the information from the passage to answer questions 21–25.

# Glaciers

Glaciers are large masses of ice, air, water, and rock. They formed in the parts of the earth where snow does not melt. The point where snow never melts is called the snow line. Above the snow line, the snow freezes hard and becomes a huge chunk of ice lying on the side of a mountain.

## Kinds of Glaciers

Glaciers can be very large. The Arctic and Antarctic, for example, are two enormous sheets of ice. Glaciers that are smaller can be found in warmer places. On high mountains, the air never rises above freezing. Smaller glaciers can form between the mountains.

## Changing the Earth

Glaciers are sometimes called rivers of ice because they move. Gravity pulls them downward off the mountain. A glacier may move a few yards or thousands of feet each year.

As a glacier moves, it takes rocks and soil along with it. This movement carves out valleys and changes the surface of the earth.

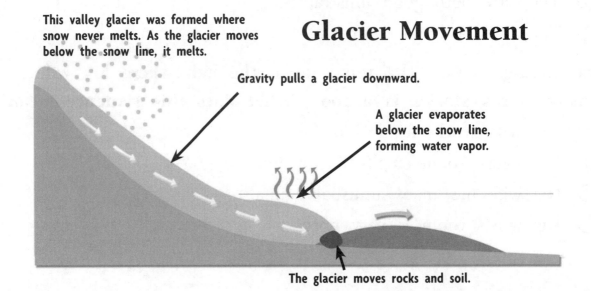

Name _____ Date _____

**21.** Which is the best summary of this passage?

Ⓐ Glaciers are sometimes called rivers of ice because they move and change.

Ⓑ Glaciers are large masses of ice that move and cause changes in the surface of the earth.

Ⓒ Glaciers are huge sheets of ice and snow that form in the mountains where ice does not melt.

Ⓓ Glaciers formed in some parts of the earth above the snow line, but they never melt.

**22.** In what area does a glacier melt?

Ⓐ above the snow line    Ⓑ in a valley

Ⓒ below the snow line    Ⓓ on the snow line

**23.** Where does the evaporated water go after it leaves the glacier?

Ⓐ It stays on the snow line.    Ⓑ It runs downhill.

Ⓒ It rises into the air.    Ⓓ On the snow line.

**24.** In what part of the passage can you learn what happens to a glacier below the snow line?

Ⓐ the first paragraph    Ⓑ **Kinds of Glaciers**

Ⓒ **Changing the Earth**    Ⓓ **Glacier Movement**

**25.** The author's main purpose in this passage is to _____.

Ⓐ give information about glaciers

Ⓑ compare the Arctic and Antarctic

Ⓒ tell an entertaining story

Ⓓ explain how to find glaciers

Name _____ Date _____

Directions: Read the passage. Then use the information from the passage to answer questions 26–30.

# Campaign Speech: July 15

### by Alonzo Santos

Greetings, citizens and friends! I am pleased to announce that I am running for mayor of this fair city on September 2nd! I need your vote, and I'll tell you why.

Our current mayor is <u>complacent</u>. He says everything in our city is just fine, but he has buried his head in the sand. If he took a good look around the city, he would see that our schools need help, our teachers need more supplies, and our classrooms have too many students and too few teachers.

If our current mayor would take a closer look around the city, he would see that crime has increased to an all-time high and our city is not as safe as it could be!

If our mayor took a good look around, he would see the potholes in our city streets and notice that our streets are crumbling!

I intend to change all this. We need more police officers on our street corners right now. We need better schools this very day, and we must fix our roadways immediately.

Let me tell you what I say.

Some people say I don't have experience. I say, "They don't know me!" Some people say that our city is fine the way it is! I say, "We need fresh ideas!" Some people say that I can't be elected because I'm only 25 and that's too young to lead. I say, "They don't know you, the voters!"

Our town needs more police officers on the streets, and we deserve it! Our town needs more teachers, and our children deserve it! Our town needs smooth, paved roads, and we deserve it!

Come with me on September 2nd. Let's make a fresh, new beginning in our town and give ourselves the city we need and want. We deserve it!

26. Based on this speech, you can tell Alonzo Santos thinks that _____.

   Ⓐ the current mayor has not done a good job
   Ⓑ every voter in the city will vote for him
   Ⓒ the people of the city are foolish
   Ⓓ no one under 25 should be elected mayor

27. Why does Alonzo Santos want to put more police officers on the streets?

   Ⓐ The schools do not have enough teachers.
   Ⓑ Many police officers recently lost their jobs.
   Ⓒ Crime has increased, and the city is not safe.
   Ⓓ The streets of the city are falling apart.

28. The passage says, "Our current mayor is <u>complacent</u>." The word <u>complacent</u> means _____.

   Ⓐ unable to change        Ⓑ pleased with the way things are
   Ⓒ ready to leave          Ⓓ prepared to meet any challenge

29. Which words best describe the character of Alonzo Santos?

   Ⓐ lazy and proud          Ⓑ ambitious and determined
   Ⓒ smart and greedy        Ⓓ honest and fair-minded

30. The speaker's main purpose in this passage is to _____.

   Ⓐ give information about the current mayor
   Ⓑ compare his city with other cities
   Ⓒ explain how to fix the city's streets
   Ⓓ persuade people to vote for him

# An Interview with Aunt Etta

When Janelle decided she wanted to make the basketball team, she interviewed her aunt Etta to get some tips on how to be a good player.

**Janelle:** When did you start playing basketball?

**Aunt Etta:** In 1957, when I was knee-high to a grasshopper, there was nothing I wanted to do more than shoot hoops in the backyard. I joined a team in the fourth grade.

**Janelle:** My mom says you were a star. How did you get so good?

**Aunt Etta:** I practiced, and I had nothing but basketball on my brain. One time in sixth grade I was at the beach with my family. The waves left foam on the sand, and the wind blew the foam up and down the beach. I pretended that the foam had a basketball, and I was trying to guard it. My legs got really strong trying to outrun the foam!

**Janelle:** Do you have any advice on how to play well?

**Aunt Etta:** When you are guarding someone, keep at her like a terrier, and never take your eyes off her waist. Players will try to trick you by faking a move, but if you only go where the player's waist goes, you'll never fall for a fake.

**Janelle:** You played guard?

**Aunt Etta:** Yes, but it was different then because forty years ago, girls only played half-court. There was a black line that divided the court in half, and you had guards and forwards. Forwards played the ball on one side of the court and tried to make points. That was the offense. The guards only played defense and tried to prevent the other side from scoring. Guards and forwards both had to stay on their own side of the court.

**Janelle:** Why did they do that?

**Aunt Etta:** People back then thought that girls were too weak to run from one end of the court to the other. At least, that's what I was told.

**Janelle:** Things have changed a lot since then!

**Aunt Etta:** Yes, they have, and aren't you glad!

Name _____ Date _____

**31.** The passage says that Aunt Etta was "knee-high to a grasshopper." What does this mean?

   Ⓐ She had legs like a grasshopper    Ⓑ She could jump really high.

   Ⓒ She was a little girl.    Ⓓ She liked to catch grasshoppers

**32.** The passage says, "Never take your eyes off her waist." Which of these sentences uses the word waist correctly?

   Ⓐ Don't waist your time on that.    Ⓑ Tie the belt around your waist.

   Ⓒ That movie was a waist of money.    Ⓓ All solid waist goes to the dump.

**33.** Aunt Etta said, "Keep at her like a terrier." What did she mean?

   Ⓐ Don't give up.    Ⓑ Stay low to the ground.

   Ⓒ Make fake moves.    Ⓓ Cheer for the player.

**34.** What did Aunt Etta do before she joined a basketball team in fourth grade?

   Ⓐ She ran after foam on the beach.    Ⓑ She played half-court games.

   Ⓒ She fell for a fake.    Ⓓ She practiced in her backyard.

**35.** The passage says, "People back then thought that girls were too weak to run." Which word from the passage means the opposite of weak?

   Ⓐ helpless    Ⓑ strong

   Ⓒ surprised    Ⓓ poor

**36.** Which is the best paraphrase of this sentence?

"Players will try to trick you by faking a move, but if you only go where the player's waist goes, you'll never fall for a fake."

   Ⓐ Players will try to trick you by moving only their waists.

   Ⓑ Go where the player goes and never fall for a fake.

   Ⓒ If you watch the player's waist, you will not be fooled by a fake.

   Ⓓ Some players fake to go one way and go the other way instead.

# Answer Sheet

Student Name _____ Date _____

Teacher Name _____ Grade _____

**Pretest**   **Midyear Test**   **Posttest**

(Circle one.)

1. Ⓐ Ⓑ Ⓒ Ⓓ
2. Ⓐ Ⓑ Ⓒ Ⓓ
3. Ⓐ Ⓑ Ⓒ Ⓓ
4. Ⓐ Ⓑ Ⓒ Ⓓ
5. Ⓐ Ⓑ Ⓒ Ⓓ
6. Ⓐ Ⓑ Ⓒ Ⓓ
7. Ⓐ Ⓑ Ⓒ Ⓓ
8. Ⓐ Ⓑ Ⓒ Ⓓ
9. Ⓐ Ⓑ Ⓒ Ⓓ
10. Ⓐ Ⓑ Ⓒ Ⓓ
11. Ⓐ Ⓑ Ⓒ Ⓓ
12. Ⓐ Ⓑ Ⓒ Ⓓ
13. Ⓐ Ⓑ Ⓒ Ⓓ
14. Ⓐ Ⓑ Ⓒ Ⓓ
15. Ⓐ Ⓑ Ⓒ Ⓓ
16. Ⓐ Ⓑ Ⓒ Ⓓ
17. Ⓐ Ⓑ Ⓒ Ⓓ
18. Ⓐ Ⓑ Ⓒ Ⓓ

19. Ⓐ Ⓑ Ⓒ Ⓓ
20. Ⓐ Ⓑ Ⓒ Ⓓ
21. Ⓐ Ⓑ Ⓒ Ⓓ
22. Ⓐ Ⓑ Ⓒ Ⓓ
23. Ⓐ Ⓑ Ⓒ Ⓓ
24. Ⓐ Ⓑ Ⓒ Ⓓ
25. Ⓐ Ⓑ Ⓒ Ⓓ
26. Ⓐ Ⓑ Ⓒ Ⓓ
27. Ⓐ Ⓑ Ⓒ Ⓓ
28. Ⓐ Ⓑ Ⓒ Ⓓ
29. Ⓐ Ⓑ Ⓒ Ⓓ
30. Ⓐ Ⓑ Ⓒ Ⓓ
31. Ⓐ Ⓑ Ⓒ Ⓓ
32. Ⓐ Ⓑ Ⓒ Ⓓ
33. Ⓐ Ⓑ Ⓒ Ⓓ
34. Ⓐ Ⓑ Ⓒ Ⓓ
35. Ⓐ Ⓑ Ⓒ Ⓓ
36. Ⓐ Ⓑ Ⓒ Ⓓ

# Individual Pretest Scoring Chart

Student Name _____ Date _____

Teacher Name _____ Grade _____

| Skill Cluster<br>Comprehension or Word Study Strategy | Item Numbers | Pretest Score |
|---|---|---|
| **1 Literary Elements**<br>Analyze Character<br>Analyze Story Elements<br>Interpret Figurative Language | 3, 4, 15, 20, 29, 31, 33 | /7 |
| **2 Text Structure and Features**<br>Analyze Text Structure and Organization<br>Use Graphic Features<br>Use Text Features | 17, 22, 23, 24 | /4 |
| **3 Relating Ideas**<br>Compare and Contrast<br>Identify Cause and Effect<br>Identify Sequence of Events | 2, 14, 27, 34 | /4 |
| **4 Inferences and Conclusions**<br>Draw Conclusions<br>Make Inferences<br>Make Predictions | 11, 12, 13, 19, 26 | /5 |
| **5 Making Judgments**<br>Evaluate Fact and Opinion<br>Evaluate Author's Purpose<br>Make Judgments | 9, 18, 25, 30 | /4 |
| **6 Distinguishing Important Information**<br>Identify Main Idea and Supporting Details<br>Summarize Information | 6, 8, 21, 36 | /4 |
| **7 Word Study**<br>Identify Synonyms, Antonyms, and Homonyms<br>Use Context Clues to Determine Word Meaning<br>Use Word Structures to Determine Word Meaning<br>Identify Multiple-Meaning Words | 1, 5, 7, 10, 16, 28, 32, 35 | /8 |
| **Total** | | /36 |
| **Percent Score** | | ___% |

# Individual Midyear Test Scoring Chart

Student Name _____  Date _____

Teacher Name _____  Grade _____

| Skill Cluster<br>Comprehension or Word Study Strategy | Item Numbers | Midyear Score |
|---|---|---|
| **1 Literary Elements**<br>Analyze Character<br>Analyze Story Elements<br>Interpret Figurative Language | 3, 4, 12, 20, 29, 31, 33 | /7 |
| **2 Text Structure and Features**<br>Analyze Text Structure and Organization<br>Use Graphic Features<br>Use Text Features | 17, 22, 23, 24 | /4 |
| **3 Relating Ideas**<br>Compare and Contrast<br>Identify Cause and Effect<br>Identify Sequence of Events | 2, 14, 27, 34 | /4 |
| **4 Inferences and Conclusions**<br>Draw Conclusions<br>Make Inferences<br>Make Predictions | 11, 13, 19, 26 | /4 |
| **5 Making Judgments**<br>Evaluate Fact and Opinion<br>Evaluate Author's Purpose<br>Make Judgments | 9, 15, 18, 25, 30 | /5 |
| **6 Distinguishing Important Information**<br>Identify Main Idea and Supporting Details<br>Summarize Information | 6, 8, 21, 26 | /4 |
| **7 Word Study**<br>Identify Synonyms, Antonyms, and Homonyms<br>Use Context Clues to Determine Word Meaning<br>Use Word Structures to Determine Word Meaning<br>Identify Multiple-Meaning Words | 1, 5, 7, 10, 16, 28, 32, 35 | /8 |
| Total | | /36 |
| Percent Score | | ___% |

156  Comprehension Strategy Assessment • Grade 4  ©2015 Benchmark Education Company, LLC

# Individual Posttest Scoring Chart

Student Name _____  Date _____

Teacher Name _____  Grade _____

| Skill Cluster<br>Comprehension or Word Study Strategy | Item Numbers | Posttest Score |
|---|---|---|
| 1  **Literary Elements**<br>    Analyze Character<br>    Analyze Story Elements<br>    Interpret Figurative Language | 3, 4, 12, 15, 20, 29, 31, 33 | /8 |
| 2  **Text Structure and Features**<br>    Analyze Text Structure and Organization<br>    Use Graphic Features<br>    Use Text Features | 17, 22, 23, 24 | /4 |
| 3  **Relating Ideas**<br>    Compare and Contrast<br>    Identify Cause and Effect<br>    Identify Sequence of Events | 2, 14, 27, 34 | /4 |
| 4  **Inferences and Conclusions**<br>    Draw Conclusions<br>    Make Inferences<br>    Make Predictions | 11, 13, 19, 26 | /4 |
| 5  **Making Judgments**<br>    Evaluate Fact and Opinion<br>    Evaluate Author's Purpose<br>    Make Judgments | 9, 18, 25, 30 | /4 |
| 6  **Distinguishing Important Information**<br>    Identify Main Idea and Supporting Details<br>    Summarize Information | 6, 8, 21, 36 | /4 |
| 7  **Word Study**<br>    Identify Synonyms, Antonyms, and Homonyms<br>    Use Context Clues to Determine Word Meaning<br>    Use Word Structures to Determine Word Meaning<br>    Identify Multiple-Meaning Words | 1, 5, 7, 10, 16, 28, 32, 35 | /8 |
| **Total** | | /36 |
| **Percent Score** | | ___% |

# Group Pretest/Midyear Test/Posttest Comparison Chart

Teacher Name _____ Grade _____

| Student Name | Pretest | | Midyear Test | | Posttest | |
|---|---|---|---|---|---|---|
| | Total Correct | Percent Score | Total Correct | Percent Score | Total Correct | Percent Score |
| | | | | | | |
| | | | | | | |
| | | | | | | |
| | | | | | | |
| | | | | | | |
| | | | | | | |
| | | | | | | |
| | | | | | | |
| | | | | | | |
| | | | | | | |
| | | | | | | |
| | | | | | | |
| | | | | | | |
| | | | | | | |
| | | | | | | |
| | | | | | | |
| | | | | | | |
| | | | | | | |
| | | | | | | |
| | | | | | | |
| | | | | | | |
| | | | | | | |
| | | | | | | |
| | | | | | | |
| | | | | | | |
| | | | | | | |

# Ongoing Strategy Assessment Record

Student Name _____

Teacher Name _____ Grade _____

| No. | Comprehension and Word Study Strategy | Reading or Listening | | Reading or Listening | |
|---|---|---|---|---|---|
| | | Date of 1st Assessment | Score | Date of 2nd Assessment | Score |
| 1–2 | Analyze Character | | | | |
| 3–4 | Analyze Story Elements | | | | |
| 5–6 | Analyze Text Structure and Organization | | | | |
| 7–8 | Compare and Contrast | | | | |
| 9–10 | Draw Conclusions | | | | |
| 11–12 | Evaluate Author's Purpose | | | | |
| 13–14 | Evaluate Fact and Opinion | | | | |
| 15–16 | Identify Cause and Effect | | | | |
| 17–18 | Identify Main Idea and Supporting Details | | | | |
| 19–20 | Identify Sequence of Events | | | | |
| 21–22 | Interpret Figurative Language | | | | |
| 23–24 | Make Inferences | | | | |
| 25–26 | Make Judgments | | | | |
| 27–28 | Make Predictions | | | | |
| 29–30 | Summarize Information | | | | |
| 31–32 | Use Graphic Features | | | | |
| 33–34 | Use Text Features | | | | |
| 35–36 | Use Word Structures to Determine Word Meaning | | | | |
| 37–38 | Use Context Clues to Determine Word Meaning | | | | |
| 39–40 | Identify Synonyms, Antonyms, and Homonyms | | | | |
| 41–42 | Identify Multiple-Meaning Words | | | | |

©2015 Benchmark Education Company, LLC

# Common Core State Standards and Virginia SOL Correlations

| Pretest | | | Midyear Test | | | Posttest | | |
| --- | --- | --- | --- | --- | --- | --- | --- | --- |
| Item | CCSS | VA SOL | Item | CCSS | VA SOL | Item | CCSS | VA SOL |
| 1. | RL.4.4 | 4.4a | 1. | RL.4.4 | 4.4b | 1. | RL.4.4 | 4.4b |
| 2. | RL.4.3 | 4.5j, 4.4 CF | 2. | RL.4.3 | 4.5j, 4.5 CF | 2. | RL.4.3 | 4.5j, 4.5 CF |
| 3. | RL.4.3 | 4.5 CF | 3. | RL.4.3 | 4.5 CF | 3. | RL.4.3 | 4.5 CF |
| 4. | RL.4.3 | 4.5e, 4.5 CF | 4. | RL.4.3 | 4.5e, 4.5 CF | 4. | RL.4.3 | 4.5e, 4.5 CF |
| 5. | RL.4.4 | 4.4a | 5. | RL.4.4 | 4.4a | 5. | RL.4.4 | 4.4a |
| 6. | RI.4.2 | 4.6d, 4.6e | 6. | RI.4.2 | 4.6d, 4.6e | 6. | RI.4.2 | 4.6d, 4.6e |
| 7. | RI.4.4 | 4.4 CF | 7. | RI.4.4 | 4.4 CF | 7. | RI.4.4 | 4.4 CF |
| 8. | RI.4.2 | 4.6d, 4.6e | 8. | RI.4.2 | 4.6d, 4.6e | 8. | RI.4.2 | 4.6d, 4.6e |
| 9. | RI.4.1 | 4.6f | 9. | RI.4.6 | 4.6f | 9. | RI.4.1 | 4.6f |
| 10. | RI.4.4 | 4.4a | 10. | RI.4.4 | 4.4 CF | 10. | RI.4.4 | 4.4a |
| 11. | RL.4.1 | 4.5h | 11. | RL.4.1 | 4.5h | 11. | RL.4.1 | 4.5h |
| 12. | RL.4.1 | 4.5h | 12. | RL.4.3 | 4.5e, 4.5 CF | 12. | RL.4.3 | 4.5e, 4.5 CF |
| 13. | RL.4.1 | 4.5h | 13. | RL.4.1 | 4.5h | 13. | RL.4.1 | 4.5h |
| 14. | RL.4.3 | 4.5 CF | 14. | RL.4.3 | 4.5 CF | 14. | RL.4.3 | 4.5 CF |
| 15. | RL.4.4 | 4.4 CF | 15. | RL.4.1 | 4.5h | 15. | RL.4.4 | 4.4 CF |
| 16. | RI.4.4 | 4.4 CF | 16. | RI.4.4 | 4.4 CF | 16. | RI.4.4 | 4.4 CF |
| 17. | RI.4.5 | 4.6g | 17. | RI.4.5 | 4.6g | 17. | RI.4.5 | 4.6g, 4.6 CF |
| 18. | RI.4.8 | 4.6h | 18. | RI.4.8 | 4.6h | 18. | RI.4.8 | 4.6h |
| 19. | RI.4.1 | 4.6f | 19. | RI.4.1 | 4.6f | 19. | RI.4.1 | 4.6f |
| 20. | RI.4.4 | 4.4 CF | 20. | RI.4.4 | 4.4 CF | 20. | RI.4.4 | 4.4 CF |
| 21. | RI.4.2 | 4.6d, 4.6e | 21. | RI.4.2 | 4.6d, 4.6e | 21. | RI.4.2 | 4.6d, 4.6e |
| 22. | RI.4.5 | 4.6g | 22. | RI.4.5 | 4.6g | 22. | RI.4.5 | 4.6g |
| 23. | RI.4.7 | 4.6a | 23. | RI.4.7 | 4.6a | 23. | RI.4.7 | 4.6a |
| 24. | RI.4.7 | 4.6a | 24. | RI.4.5 | 4.6a | 24. | RI.4.5 | 4.6a |
| 25. | RI.4.6 | 4.6c | 25. | RI.4.6 | 4.6c | 25. | RI.4.6 | 4.6c |
| 26. | RL.4.1 | 4.5h | 26. | RL.4.1 | 4.5h | 26. | RL.4.1 | 4.5h |
| 27. | RL.4.3 | 4.5j | 27. | RL.4.3 | 4.5j | 27. | RL.4.3 | 4.5j |
| 28. | RL.4.4 | 4.4a | 28. | RL.4.4 | 4.4a | 28. | RL.4.4 | 4.4a |
| 29. | RL.4.3 | 4.5 CF | 29. | RL.4.3 | 4.5 CF | 29. | RL.4.3 | 4.5 CF |
| 30. | RL.4.6 | 4.5a, 4.5b | 30. | RL.4.6 | 4.5a, 4.5b | 30. | RL.4.6 | 4.5a, 4.5b |
| 31. | RI.4.4 | 4.5 CF, 4.4 CF | 31. | RI.4.4 | 4.4 CF | 31. | RL.4.4 | 4.4 CF, 4.5 CF |
| 32. | RI.4.4 | 4.4 CF | 32. | RI.4.4 | 4.4 CF | 32. | RL.4.4 | 4.4 CF |
| 33. | RI.4.4 | 4.4 CF | 33. | RI.4.4 | 4.4 CF | 33. | RL.4.4 | 4.4 CF |
| 34. | RI.4.3 | 4.4 CF | 34. | RI.4.3 | 4.4 CF | 34. | RL.4.3 | 4.4 CF |
| 35. | RI.4.4 | 4.4b | 35. | RI.4.4 | 4.4b | 35. | RL.4.4 | 4.4b |
| 36. | RI.4.2 | 4.6e | 36. | RI.4.2 | 4.6d, 4.6e | 36. | RL.4.2 | 4.5d, 4.5 CF |